PERGAMON INSTITUTE OF ENGLISH
(NEW YORK)

Materials for Language Practice

COMMUNICATING IN
ENGLISH

EXAMPLES AND MODELS

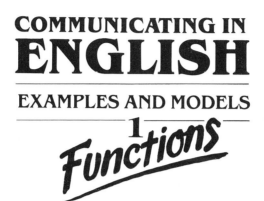

COMMUNICATING IN ENGLISH: EXAMPLES AND MODELS *is a three-volume series for high intermediate and advanced students of English as a Second or Foreign Language. The three volumes, written by Walter Matreyek and published by Pergamon Press, are:*
>   Book 1: Functions
>   Book 2: Notions
>   Book 3: Situations

Other textbooks already published in our Materials for Language Practice Series for the student of American English:

ENGLISH AS AN INTERNATIONAL LANGUAGE: Eva S. Weiner and Larry E. Smith
A workbook which focuses on writing activities, which are also used as a base for the practice of the other skills. Its strong international flavor promotes students' understanding of different cultures.
0 08 030322 6f

PINT'S PASSAGES FOR AURAL COMPREHENSION: John Pint
Two books providing an ingenious combination of aural comprehension and cloze exercises.

TWENTIETH CENTURY NEWS
0 08 028620 8f
0 08 029430 8a Cassette kit (*book and cassette,*

TELEPHONE TALK
0 08 028621 6f
0 08 029455 3a Cassette kit (*book and cassette*)

READING SKILLS FOR THE FUTURE: Susan Lebauer
A systematic text designed to improve the reading skills of the student or professional; centred around the theme of energy resources.
0 08 028619 4f

TALK AND LISTEN: Richard Via and Larry E. Smith
English as an international language via drama techniques. Emphasis is placed on developing grammatical acceptability and social appropriateness. Practice goes all the way from simple dialogues to detailed roleplays.
0 08 030323 4f *Students' Book*
0 08 029448 0f *Teachers' Book*

YOSHI GOES TO NEW YORK: John Battaglia and Marilyn Fisher
Unscripted conversations with a businessman in New York is the story line. Authentic conversations and authentic materials combine to provide a course with wide appeal to all students regardless of nationality.
0 08 028648 8f
0 08 028665 8a Cassette kit (*book and cassette*)

COMMUNICATING IN ENGLISH

EXAMPLES AND MODELS

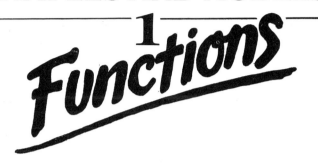

1 Functions

International Edition

Walter Matreyek

PERGAMON PRESS

New York · Oxford · Toronto · Sydney · Paris · Frankfurt

U.S.A.	Pergamon Press Inc., Maxwell House, Fairview Park, Elmsford, New York 10523, U.S.A.
U.K.	Pergamon Press Ltd., Headington Hill Hall, Oxford OX3 0BW, England
CANADA	Pergamon Press Canada Ltd., Suite 104, 150 Consumers Road, Willowdale, Ontario M2J 1P9, Canada
AUSTRALIA	Pergamon Press (Aust.) Pty. Ltd., P.O. Box 544, Potts Point, N.S.W. 2011, Australia
FRANCE	Pergamon Press SARL, 24 rue des Ecoles, 75240 Paris, Cedex 05, France
FEDERAL REPUBLIC OF GERMANY	Pergamon Press GmbH, Hammerweg 6, D-6242 Kronberg Taunus, Federal Republic of Germany

Copyright © 1983 Pergamon Press Inc.
Illustrations © 1983 Ian Kellas

First edition 1983

Library of Congress Cataloguing in Publication Data

Matreyek, Walter.
Communicating in English.
(Materials for language practice)
"A Flamm/Northam book" — T.p. verso.
Includes index.
Contents: 1. Interpersonal functions — 2. Semantic functions — 3. Conversation techniques, topics and situations.
1. English language — Text-books for foreigners.
2. English language — Spoken English. I. Title. II. Series.
PE1128.M354   1983   428.2'4   82-15006

British Library Cataloguing in Publication Data

Matreyek, Walter
Communicating in English: examples and models.
(Materials for language practice)
Vol. 1. Functions
1. English language — Text-books for foreigners
I. Title   II. Series
428.2'4   PE1128
ISBN 0 08 028616 X

A Flamm/Northam book

Contents

CHAPTER 6 ASKING ABOUT/STATING   1

CHAPTER 7 ASKING ABOUT/STATING   2

Students' Introduction

You have to learn many things when you learn a new language. The first things you probably studied were pronunciation, grammar and vocabulary. But these are not enough. Another important thing to learn is the language used to:

Say greetings and farewells

Apologize and forgive

Tell someone to be quiet

Ask for or offer help

Ask for or give examples

Ask about or express impatience or anger

Ask about or state opinions

and many others . . .

These things are called **interpersonal functions** because we do these things in relation to other people. We use the above and other functions many, many times in our everyday lives.

This book will help you to learn the language of these functions. You will learn polite and more informal ways of doing these things. You will also learn some ways of doing them that you need to be careful about. If you're not careful with the ways that are marked with an asterisk (*), you may say something a little strange, or you may insult someone without really meaning to.

You will learn these interpersonal functions actively. You will need to read, think about, discuss and **act**. The acting part may be difficult at first, but it will become easier as you get used to the book and other people in the class. By the end of your English classes, we hope that you will be able to recognize these things in your everyday life easily and that you'll be able to use this book to help you by yourself.

Good luck, and I hope you enjoy learning interpersonal functions in English.

Walter Matreyek

Seattle, Washington, USA

Teachers' Introduction

This is a text in functional English for intermediate and advanced students. It focuses on the language people use in everyday life communication. It is designed for people who have some background in English, but who also have gaps, lacks of variety or other problems in using English to communicate in everyday life.

This text is written to develop active, aware, and independent learners. It is a performance-oriented text, so students need to read, think about, discuss and practice and perform the Examples, Models, and Suggested Activities in each lesson. In doing so, they actively internalize the language related to the interpersonal functions in the book so that they can use them in everyday life. The Preliminary Activities in Appendix 1 and the Suggested Techniques in Appendix 2 will help to develop and promote this active learning.

In addition, the text helps to develop aware learners: people who can recognize a particular situation and what is being called for as a response to the situation. Students begin to think about how to make an appropriate desired initiative or response, rather than how to come up with a grammatically correct sentence or question. Lastly, the present text is one that students can learn to use by themselves, independently, outside of class or after class has finished. If we can help students to become active, aware, and independent learners, we are helping them to become people who can use English to accomplish what they want to in English.

Format of Lessons

Each lesson is divided into three sections: Examples, Models and Suggested Activities. Examples are words, expressions, sentences or questions which show how the particular function in each lesson is used in everyday life. Models are conversation and discussion excerpts which place some of the examples in larger everyday contexts. Suggested Activities are problem-solving situations where the students have to apply what they've just learned in the Examples and Models sections in less structured ways.

There are three things to keep in mind when using the text:

1 *Not all possible examples of the function are given in each lesson.* Rather, the examples are limited to the most common and direct ones. This is because the text would

soon become too long and unmanageable if all the subtle and indirect ways to express the function were given.

2 *Students will need to understand when and how to use various examples.* They need to understand which forms are polite, which are more informal or colloquial, and which forms they need to be careful about. In many lessons, informal forms are given first, then polite ones are given. Other lessons are arranged in other ways. Throughout the text, forms which can easily be misunderstood or misconstrued are marked with an asterisk (*). As the teacher, you will need to give students some added information about the appropriateness of particular forms with particular people in particular situations until they develop the awareness of the language to do this by themselves.

3 *You should not try to work through the book sequentially, lesson by lesson.* Rather, you should select certain lessons to work on using the Contents section of the book as a check-list. Each lesson has the same format to help in selecting lessons as needed. However, since each lesson has the same format, you will need to vary the way you work with different lessons. You will find a number of suggested techniques and activities in the next section of this introduction, and detailed explanations of these techniques and activities in Appendix 2.

Using this Book

When you work on a lesson, I suggest you use the following four stages:
1   Reading
2   Discussion
3   Practice or Performance
4   Reflection

By using these four steps, you will make maximum use of students' learning time and energy.

1   Reading

After deciding on a particular lesson, ask students to read the Examples and Models sections before the next class. During the reading assignment, students have a chance to think and guess about the meanings and usages of various forms in the Examples and Models. These thoughts and guesses will be confirmed or refuted and revised in later stages. Some students find this step difficult at first, because it involves thoughtful reading. However, it is necessary in order to help students develop the ability to understand and accurately guess about meaning and usage later, both inside and outside or after class.

2   Discussion

In class, then, you can read and discuss the Examples and Models with the students. First, read the Examples aloud in a way which is appropriate to related imagined situations. Next, read the Models aloud in a way appropriate to the given situations. The reading aloud is followed by discussion of the Examples and Models. In this discussion, you can touch upon a number of things:

(a) the meanings of words and expressions that students still have questions about,
(b) the context of the Examples and Models: the time, place, people and people's probable intentions and feelings,

(c) the politeness or informality with which things are said. Also, you will need to talk about the forms that they need to be careful about and why (the ones marked with asterisks *),

(d) the intonation, stress and quality of voice with which things are probably said,

(e) what they themselves might think, feel, say and do in similar situations.

Discussions can range from teacher-guided ones to ones where students are working in their own groups with the teacher acting as consultant. You need to be careful not to belabor this stage, as students might begin to lose interest and enthusiasm. You need not talk about all the Examples and Models in great depth. Rather, you're aiming for understanding of major things: enough to allow them to practice and perform in the next stage.

3 Practice and Performance

This is the stage where students act upon their understandings. You can use some of the following techniques in practicing and performing the Examples, Models and Suggested Activities. (Detailed explanations are given in Appendix 2.)

Examples: Interpretative Reading; Skits/Improvised Role-Plays.
Models: Interpretative Reading: Talking and Listening; Puppet Shows; Tape-Recording and VTR.
Suggested Activities: Skits/Improvised Role-playing; Interpretative Reading; Puppet Shows: Tape-Recording and VTR

An important thing in this stage is that students are on their feet and applying the things they understood and learned in the first two stages. They will need to discuss the situations in the Suggested Activities so they understand them. Their performance of the Suggested Activities is the "test" of their ability to recognize the need for and the use of the functions.

4 Reflection

This last stage gives students the chance to look back and comment on their experience. Some may still have questions; some may comment on the learning process and how they felt; some may have suggestions about how to do things differently. The reflection should help give a feeling of completeness, sharing, and confidence so that people are ready to move on to the next lesson. With the next lesson, the four-stage process begins again.

General Suggestions

This four-stage process of reading, discussion, practice/performance and reflection should not be an overly long and complicated thing. It will go slowly at first, but you will be able to go more quickly after students get used to it.

It might also help to keep the following suggestions in mind:

(a) Both you and the students will need a willingness to try something new and different. At first people may be shy, and things will be halting and confusing. The preliminary activities, which work on activity, instruction following, and imagination, will help make everyone a little more comfortable about the process.

(b) Don't ask students to do something you yourself wouldn't do or something that goes against cultural norms. For example, don't ask Arab students to play roles involving heavy drinking. Doing so many cause conflicts with personal beliefs.

(c) In the practice and performance stages, help students to understand and act out the situation and people's thoughts and feelings by referring to their own experiences. Some of the preliminary activities in Appendix 1 work specifically on this.

(d) Don't go through the book sequentially lesson by lesson. Use the Contents section as a way of selecting particular functions to work on. The students themselves can and should be consulted in deciding which to work on.

A note on usage

You will find in this text that I have taken some liberties that are rarely, if ever, seen in an ESL/EFL textbook. To reproduce that authentic colloquial speech of present-day Americans I have used the spelling conventions used by authors of fiction for this purpose. Thus, you will see some -*ing* forms given in examples of very informal speech functions with an apostrophe replacing the final g. In this same vein, you will occasionally see *you* written as *ya, What are you . . .* transcribed as *Wha'cha . . .,* and *Come on* as *C'mon.* For the most part, however, standard spelling has been used throughout the book. Also to reflect informal usage, the usual structural markers in Yes/No questions are deleted, as in *You catching a cold?* instead of the standard English *Are you catching a cold?*

Native speakers of English commonly use pause fillers or hesitation devices in their conversation. These have been transcribed, again adhering to practice in fiction, as *uhmmm . . ., hmmm . . .,* and *uh.* In addition, I have included meaningful sounds in their accepted transcriptions such as *shhh* and *yuck.*

Everyday Functions

CHAPTER 1

Functions 1

1 Greetings and Farewells

A EXAMPLES (Read, Discuss and Practice)

Greetings

A Hi, Larry
   Hey, Alice!
   Hello, Bob.
   Good morning, Mr. Kim.
   Good afternoon.
   Good evening.

How's it going?
How're you doin?
How are things with you?
Long time no see.
How are you?

B Fine thanks.
   O.K.
   So-so.
   Not bad.
   I'm fine, thank you.
   Very well, thank you.

And how're you doin'?
How about you?
And you?
And how are you?

Farewells

A Bye (Bye-bye).
   See you later.
   See you again.
   Take it easy.
   Take care of yourself.
   Goodbye.

B Bye.
   Hope so.
   Sure thing.
   You, too.
   Goodbye.

1

B MODELS (Read, Discuss and Perform the following model dialogues)

1 *Two friends pass each other in the street.*
   F1: Hey, Jim. How's it going?
   F2: Oh, hi, Nancy. O.K. How're you doin'? Long time no see.
   F1: Yeah, it has been a long time. Too long. Unfortunately, I'm in kind of a rush right now . . .
   F2: So am I. Catch you some other time, huh?
   F2: Yeah. Let's get together sometime. Take it easy.
   F2: You, too.

2 *Two acquaintances meet in a supermarket and stop to talk.*
   A1: Hello, Stan. How have you been?
   A2: Oh, hi, Luanne. Not bad, thank you. How about you?
   A1: Pretty good. Today's shopping day, is it?
   A2: Yeah. I have to buy a few things for dinner tonight.
   A1: Uhmm. . .so do I. By the way, have you heard about Fred!
   (a few minutes later)
   A2: . . .that's really interesting about Fred. Well, I'd better finish my shopping. It's been really nice talking with you, Luanne.
   A1: I've enjoyed it too. I hope we run into each other again.
   A2: Yeah, I do, too. Take care, O.K.?
   A1: Yeah, you, too.

3 *A man who wants to check some books out of the library goes to the librarian's desk.*
   L : Good afternoon, Sir. Can I help you?
   M: Good afternoon. I'd like to check out these books if I may.
   L: Yes, of course. Here, I'll take them. May I see your library card?
   M: Yes. Here it is. . .

L: O.K., sir. Here you are. These will be due the 31st of the month. Enjoy your reading, and have a nice day.

M: You, too.

C SUGGESTED ACTIVITIES (Discuss and Perform)

Imagine the following situations. What would you do?

1 You unexpectedly meet a friend in the drug store. You haven't seen each other for at least a couple of months.
2 A student meets his/her professor on the way to the library one afternoon.
3 Two office workers meet by the copy machine at work. They know each other only slightly.

2 Welcoming

A EXAMPLES (Read, Discuss and Practice)

Welcome!
Welcome home!
Welcome back to class!
Welcome to Brownsville!
Let me welcome you to our beautiful city!
I'd like to welcome you to your first meeting of Weight Losers.

B MODELS (Read, Discuss and Perform the following model dialogues)

1 *A student, Stan, returns to class after being in the hospital. He is greated by his fellow students.*
   S1: Hey, guys, look who's back!
   S2: Hey! It's Stan!
   Stan: Hy, you guys.
   S3: Yeah, welcome back, Stan. It's nice to have you back.
   Stan: Thanks. I'm glad to be back.

2 *A branch manager is meeting a vice-president at the airport.*
   BM: Good afternoon, Mr. Browning. Welcome to Martinstown!
   VP: Thank you, Les.
   BM: How was your flight?
   VP: Oh, not bad. It was a little rough in places, but. . .

3 *A small town major sees some tourists in the town square.*
   M: Hello. You seem to be enjoying our little town. Let me welcome you to Gold Dust. I'm Thomas Jones, Mayor.
   T1: Thank you, Mr. Jones. It seems like a nice town.
   T2: Yeah, I think so, too. How old is the town?
   M: We're 157 years old this year. . .

C SUGGESTED ACTIVITIES (Discuss and Perform)

What would you do in the following situations?

1 A host at a party is greeting and welcoming people to the party.
2 You are the owner of a hotel in a small resort town. Some guests come into the hotel.
3 You're meeting a friend, who is returning from a trip, at the airport.

3 Introductions

Self-Introductions

A EXAMPLES (Read, Discuss and Practice)

A Hi. My name is Eddie.
Hi. I'm Liant. What's your name?
Hello. My name is Paul, Paul Goodwin.
I'd like to introduce myself. I'm Bob
Peterman.
May I introduce myself? My name is Ralph
Winston.

B Nice to meet you.
Pleased to meet you.   My name is Phyllis Ameryl.
I'm glad to meet you.   I'm Connie Michaels.
How do you do.

B MODELS (Read, Discuss and Perform the following model dialogues)

1 *A man begins to talk with a woman at a party.*
   M: Hi. My name is Joshua Green. I saw you standing here alone, and I thought I might join you a moment.
   W: Hello, Mr. Green. It's nice to meet you. My name is Lori Stevens. Please call me Lori.
   M: O.K., Lori. Please call me Josh. Are you a friend of Dick and Tracy's?
   W: Yes, I am. I've known them for some ten years now. And you?

2 *Two married couples meet and begin talking at a camp-ground.*
   H1: This sure is a beautiful lake, isn't it.

H2: It sure is.

H1: We just got here a couple of hours ago, and have been taking a drive around the lake. The countryside is also nice.

H2: Is that so? We'll have to try that. By the way, My name's Harold Stevens. This is my wife, Rita.

H1: Pleased to meet you. I'm Milton Westlake — call me Milt. My wife's name is Arlene.

W1: How do you do.

W2: Nice to meet you. Where are you folks from?

Introducing People to Other People

A EXAMPLES (Read, Discuss and Practice)

A Henry, this is Alison Turnbull.
Marge, this is a good friend of mine,
Bob Jones.
Mary, I'd like you to meet Phil Sweet.
Lisa, I'd like to introduce you to Tom
Martin.
Steve, may I introduce you to Ralph
Butterman.

B Glad to meet you.
I'm happy to meet you, Bob.
It's nice to meet you.
It's a pleasure to meet you.
How do you do, Mr Butterman.

C Nice to meet you, too.
Sam here.
It's my pleasure.
How do you do.

B MODELS (Read, Discuss and Perform the following model dialogues)

1 *The host and hostess at a party introduce two guests.*

H: . . .so, if we move, it'll be next year. Hey, it looks like Ann is talking with Jill Martin. Do you know her?

G: No, I'm afraid I don't.

H: In that case, let me introduce you to each other. I think you'll like each other.

(They go to where Ann and Jill are talking.)

H: Excuse me, Ann. Edwin here says that he hasn't met Jill. I'd like to introduce them.

H: Oh, that's a good idea, Marvin.

H: Jill, this is Edwin Needman. Edwin, I'd like you to meet Jill Martin. She's a friend of Ann's from college.

J: I'm pleased to meet you, too, Mr. Needman.

E: Please call me Ed.

J: O.K., Ed.

H: Jill works with the Public Health Service.

E: Is that so. It sounds like interesting work.

2 Two businessmen are talking and one sees a friend.

BM1: . . . so, business is looking pretty good. Hey, that's Martha Cowell over there. You know her, don't you?

BM2: No. I've never met her.

BM1: Well, then. Let's go over and I'll introduce you.

(They go to where Martha is standing.)

BM1: Martha! How're you doing? It's been a long time!

M: George! What a surprise seeing you here.

BM1: Roger tells me you've never met. Martha, this is Roger Harmon. Roger, I'd like you to meet Martha Cowell.

BM2: How do you do, Ms. Cowell.

M: It's nice to meet you, Mr . . . I'm sorry, I didn't quite catch your name . . .

BM2: Harmon. But please call me Roger.

M: O.K. Roger. And call me Martha. What business are you in?

BM2: I'm with Lightship Industries. We make gliders.

BM1: Martha's with Control Systems, Inc. As you know, they make aerospace guidance systems . . .

BM2: I know. What part of the company are you in, Martha?

C SUGGESTED ACTIVITIES (Discuss and Perform)

How could the following situations be handled?

1 You are a member of a hobby club, and your club is having a membership drive. You are at an open house, and you see some people come in. You want to interest them in the club.

2 You're walking down the street with your parents, and you see an acquaintance approaching from the other direction.

3 A businessman and businesswoman are having lunch at a restaurant. She sees a colleague come in and wants to introduce the man to her colleague.

4 Getting Attention

A EXAMPLES (Read, Discuss and Practice)

Hey!
Hey,
Excuse me . . .
Pardon me . . .
Oh, Sir!
Oh, Miss!
*Hey, you!

B MODELS (Read, Discuss and Perform the following model dialogues)

1 *Two people waiting for a bus see a friend across the street.*
   P1: . . . and so I told him that . . .
   P2: Hold on a second. Isn't that June across the street?
   P1: Yeah, it looks like her. Hey June! Where're ya goin'?
   F: Mike! Steve! How're you guys?

2 *A shop-clerk notices a customer has forgotten her purse.*
   SC: Oh, Miss!
   C: Yes?
   SC: You forgot your purse.
   C: Oh, I did, didn't I. Thank you.
   SC: That's quite all right.

3 *A man is walking behind another man on the street.*
   M1: Excuse me. I think you dropped this.
   M2: Oh, did I? I guesse I did. Thank you.
   M1: You're welcome.

C SUGGESTED ACTIVITIES (Discuss and Perform)

If you were in the following situations, what would you do?

1 You are riding a crowded bus, and a pregnant woman gets on.
2 A waitress in an expensive restaurant notices that a customer has left a package behind.
3 A man and woman get out of their car at a scenic spot along a highway. The woman goes to the side of the road, looks out and calls to the man.

5 Regulating Other Peoples Speech

Asking for Repetition and Repeating

A EXAMPLES (Read, Discuss and Practice)

Asking for Repetition

Huh? What?
Say again?
Excuse me? Pardon me?
I beg your pardon?
What did you say?
What was that you said?
Please repeat that.
Could you say that again, please
Would you mind repeating that.

Repeating

I said, "I don't care."
I asked, "Where was he hiding?"
I said that I didn't see them.
I asked if you were ill.
I asked you where you're going.
What I said was, "I'm tired of working there."

B MODELS (Read, Discuss and Perform the following model dialogues)

1 *Two people are talking. One is not paying close attention.*

P1: ... so, while I was shopping the other day, I saw this on sale and got it for half price How do you like it?

P2: Huh? Oh, excuse me, but I was thinking about something else just now. What did you ask me?

P1: I was saying that I just bought this blouse on sale, and I asked you how you like it. Are you O.K.? You look a little worried about something.

P2: Oh, yeah, I'm O.K. That is a really nice blouse . . .

2 *A businesswoman is talking with her boss in his office.*

B: . . . in any case, Althea, the reason why I called you here is to congratulate you on becoming the new sales manager.

BW. Excuse me, Mr. Thompson. What did you just say? Would you mind repeating that?

B: I said, "Congratulations on becoming the new sales manager." The Board of Directors has been very impressed with your work and felt you could handle a little more responsiblility.

BW: Why, thank you, Mr. Thompson. I'm sure I can do a good job.

Speed and Volume

A EXAMPLES (Read, Discuss and Practice)

Speed

Please speak a little more slowly.
Could you please speak slowly.
Would you mind not speaking quite so fast.
*Slow down a little, will you.
*How about slowing down a little, O.K.?

Volume

Please speak a little louder.
Could you please speak a little louder?
Would you mind speaking a little more loudly.
I'm sorry, I can't hear you.
*I can't hear a word you're saying.
*Speak up, will you.

B MODELS (Read, Discuss and Perform the following model dialogues)

1 *A man is calling from a pay-telephone on a busy street.*
   W: ... and she was arrested last night ...
   M: What did you say? I can't hear you.
   W: I said, "she was arrested last night."
   M: I'm sorry, Mary. It's really noisy here. Can you please speak a little louder.
   W: I SAID, "BETTY WAS ARRESTED LAST NIGHT." CAN YOU HEAR ME NOW?
   M: Yeah, now I can hear you. What did you say?

2 *A foreign businessman is talking with an American colleaguie.*
   AC: ... the model I showed you last night has all these money-saving features and more ...
   FBM: Excuse me, Chris, but I'm having a hard time following what you're saying. How about speaking a little louder, and a little more slowly, too, if you don't mind.
   AC: I'm sorry. I sometimes forget that English is not your first language. How about we get out of the factory and go back to my office. I think we've seen everything here.
   FBM: Fine with me. I hope it's a little quieter there ...

C SUGGESTED ACTIVITIES (Discuss and Perform)

How might you handle the following situations?

1 You are talking with a friend about his family. You begin to think about something else, and you suddenly find that he's waiting for an answer to a question.
2 You are in a new city, and you're asking a person for directions at a busy bus-stop. You're having a hard time understanding and hearing the person.
3 You're talking with a friend long-distance on the telephone. The connection is bad.
4 You're trying to talk with a friend who always talks a mile a minute. You want him to slow down.

6 Thanking / Gratitude

A EXAMPLES (Read, Discuss and Practice)

Thanking
Thanks.
Thank you.
Thank you for calling.
That was very kind of you.
It was very nice of you to help me.
How can I ever thank you?

I can't thank you enough.
I really appreciate what you've done for
my family.
Can I show my appreciation by buying
you an ice cream?

Responding to Thanks
You're welcome.
It's O.K.
Don't mention it.
That's quite all right.
Thank you
No need to thank me.
It was my pleasure.

B MODELS (Read, Discuss and Perform the following model dialogues)

1 *A man is talking with a friend on the telephone.*
   M: Well, Archy, thanks a lot for telling me the good news.
   F: Oh, that's O.K. I thought you'd be interested.
   M: I am. I wish both of you the best of luck in the future.
   F: Why, thank you. Well, O.K., I'd better hang up now.
   M: Yeah, we've been on the phone quite a while, haven't we. Take it easy, huh? Thanks again for calling.
   F: Oh, my pleasure. See you soon. Bye.

2 *A woman is talking with her son's high-school principal.*
   P : Well, Mrs. Quitman, it looks like your son's going to be a Harvard man next year.
   W: Dr. Franklin, how can we ever thank you? You've done so much to help our boy.
   P: No need to thank me. It's part of my job, after all.
   W: Well, thank you again anyway. We really appreciate the time and interest you've taken . . .

3 *An elderly woman is talking with a young boy who helped her.*
   EW: Michael, it was very kind of you to carry my groceries for me. Thank you very much.
   YB: Aw, it's O.K., Mrs. Phillips. I know it's pretty hard for you. It's no trouble for me.
   EW: Let's see. Can I show my appreciation by offering you some cookies and milk?
   YB: Wow! Really? That's great. Thanks.
   EW: O.K. Well, come in. You're a good friend . . .

C SUGGESTED ACTIVITIES (Discuss and Perform)

What would you do if you were in the following situations?

1 You are shopping and carrying a lot of packages. You drop one, and another person picks it up for you.
2 A friend invites you to a party. You accept the invitation.
3 You work in an office, and you are very busy. You have to proof-read a long report before quitting time. An office-mate offers to help you. You gladly accept the offer.

7 Requests and Offers

Requests

A EXAMPLES (Read, Discuss and Practice)

Making Requests

Talk to him, O.K.?
Proof-read this for me, will you?
Please let me have that book when you're finished.
Can you help me with this?
Could you please turn down the radio a little?
May I open the window?
May I please have a glass of water?
May I ask you to mail this for me on your way to work?
Would you mind watching this for me a few minutes?
Would it be possible to type this letter before you go home?
If I can make a request, I'd like to hear some classical music.

Asking for Requests

Is there anything I can get you?
Do you want something?
Do you have any requests?
Does anyone have any requests?
Are there any requests?

B MODELS (Read, Discuss and Perform the following model dialogues)

1 *A woman is talking on the telephone at home.*
   W: Just a minute, Patty. I can't hear you. Bill's watching the football game on TV. Bill . . . turn down the TV a little, will you?
   H: What?
   W: Can you turn down the volume on the TV a little?
   H: Yeah, yeah . . . O.K. Is this better?
   W: A little . . . Can you turn it down a little more? I'm on the phone . . .
   H: Oh, sure. Sorry.

2 *A man calls the waitress at a restaurant.*
   M: Excuse me, Miss. Can I please have another glass of water?
   W: Of course. I'll bring it in a moment.
   (A few minutes later)
   W: I'm sorry to take so long. Here you are. How's your meal?
   M: It's fine.
   W: Is there anything else I can get you?
   M: No. This is enough. I'd like to have the check, though.
   W: Yes, Sir. I'll bring it in a few minutes.

3 *A young girl talks with an elderly couple at a bus-station.*
  G: Excuse me, would you mind watching my bag for me a minute? I have to use the bathroom . . .
  M: Of course, young lady. We'll watch it for you.
  (She returns)
  G: Thank you very much.
  W: You're quite welcome.

Offers

A EXAMPLES (Read, Discuss and Practice)

Offering

Here, have a seat.
Here, take some sugar.
Please have a piece of candy.
Can I get you some coffee?
Would you like to use my pen?
Do you want me to help you?
Would you like me to type that letter for you?

Here, let me open that.
I'll do that, if you want me to.
How about another piece of pie?
How'd you like me to bring you back a sandwich?

Accepting

Yes.
Thank you.
Please.
Would you mind?
If it's no trouble for you.
That's very kind of you.

Declining

No, thank you.
That's not necessary.
That's O.K.
Thanks, but it's O.K.
Thanks but no thanks.

B MODELS (Read, Discuss and Perform the following model dialogues)

1 *An elderly woman gets on a bus, and a young man offers his seat.*
  YM: Excuse me, Ma'am. Here, please take my seat.
  EW: Thank you, young man.

2 *A woman is visiting her friend Marge's house.*
  M: Hi, Marge. Come in. Here, let me take your coat.
  W: Thanks, Phil. Is Sue back from shopping yet?
  M: Not yet, but she should be soon. Can I get you some coffee?
  W: No, thanks. I've given up coffee. It makes me too nervous.
  M: Yeah. Same for me. How about some herb tea?
  W: That sounds fine. Thank you.
  M: O.K. I'll be back in just a minute. Sit down.

3 *A woman and her teen-age son are walking home from the store.*
  W: Tommy, look at that poor old man carrying that heavy package. Why don't you go over and offer to help him?

15

S: He looks like he's doing O.K.

W: Go on, offer to carry it for him. Be nice to old people.

S: Oh, all right . . . Excuse me, Mister. Would you like me to help you with that?

M: Why, thank you, son. It's getting pretty heavy for me.

C SUGGESTED ACTIVITIES (Discuss and Perform)

What would you do if you were in the following situations?

1 You are at a friend's house talking about your vacation plans. You're becoming thirsty.
2 A friend is visiting, and you're going to put a record on the stereo. You want to know if he has any particular requests.
3 You are at an elderly aunt's house. She is trying to read the newspaper, but the print is too small for her.
4 Two people are walking their dogs. One has to use the rest-room.

8 Excuses

Asking to be Excused and Excusing

A EXAMPLES (Read, Discuss and Practice)

Asking to be Excused	Excusing
Excuse me.	That's O.K.
Pardon me.	It's all right.
I beg your pardon	It's nothing.
I must excuse myself.	No problem.
Please forgive me.	

I have to excuse myself a moment.	Go ahead.
May I be excused?	O.K. with me.
Can I be excused from class today?	Of course.
Permit me to excuse myself.	You're excused.
I'm sorry, but I must call my office.	You may be excused.

B MODELS (Read, Discuss and Perform the following model dialogues)

1 *Two people are talking. One coughs quite a bit.*
   P1:   . . . I sent him a letter last week. *(coughs)* Excuse me.
   P2:   Has he gotten it yet?
   P1:   It seems not. *(Coughs again)* Excuse me again.
   P2:   Are you O.K.? You catching a cold or something?
   P1:   *(coughs)* Please forgive me. I think I am getting a cold . . .

2 *A woman bumps into a man at a museum.*
   W :   Oh, I beg your pardon. I wasn't watching where I was going.
   M: That's quite all right.

3 *A student talks with her teacher before class.*
   S: Excuse me Dr. Johnson . . .
   T: Yes. What can I do for you?
   S: May I be excused from class this afternoon? I'm not feeling very well, and I want to go to the infirmary.
   T: Of course. You're excused. I hope you feel better afterwards.

Asking for and Giving an Excuse

A EXAMPLES (Read, Discuss and Practice)

Asking for an Excuse
Why are you late?
How come you didn't show up?
What's your excuse?
What do you have to say for yourself?
What is it this time?

Giving an Excuse
I'm sorry, but the bus was late.
My excuse is that my car had a flat tire.
I couldn't help it . . . I was just too busy to call.

Accepting
Well, I guess it's O.K.
O.K. Let's forget about it.
All right. You're excused.
Well, it's O.K. this time, but there had better not be a next time.

Rejecting
No excuses!
Don't give me any excuses.
I'm tired of your excuses.
That's a lousy excuse.
Think of something better.

B MODELS (Read, Discuss and Perform the following model dialogues)

1 *The head nurse at a hospital is talking with a trainee nurse.*
   HN: Miss Young. This is the third time you're late this week. What's your excuse this time?
   TN: I'm sorry, Mrs. Chan. I didn't hear the alarm.
   HN: And what do you expect me to do about it, Miss Young?
   TN: I'm sorry. I don't know. Maybe I'm not meant to be a nurse . . .

2 *A man is having an argument with a garage mechanic.*
   M: . . . You've had my car for two weeks now. Aren't you finished?
   GM: Sorry, Mr. Johnson. We've been busy lately, and two men are out with the flu . . .
   M: I'm tired of your excuses. Every time I come it's a different one. I want my car by Friday, and no more excuses.
   GM: Listen, man, you can have it right now for all I care . . .

C SUGGESTED ACTIVITIES (Discuss and Perform)

How might the following situations be handled?

1 You are talking with someone, and you suddenly have a loud hiccough.
2 A man is talking with friends at a party, and he suddenly feels a little sick.
3 Your best friend promised to meet you at a restaurant at 6 p.m. It is now 6.45 and he has just come in.
4 A young boy was supposed to clean the yard around the house, but he went to play with friends instead. He comes home, and his mother is angry.

9 Apologizing / Forgiving

A EXAMPLES (Read, Discuss and Practice)

Apologizing

I'm sorry.
Sorry about that.
I beg your pardon.
I apologize.
I'm sorry that I couldn't come on time.
I apologize for saying that.
I must apologize for my son's rudeness.
Please forgive me for having thrown your book away.

Forgiving

It's O.K.
Forget about it.
Don't worry about it.
No problem.
I forgive you.
I accept your apologies.
You don't have to apologize.
There's no need to apologize.

Rejecting an Apology

Are you really sorry?
I don't believe you're sorry.
You're not really sorry.
Don't say you're sorry.
I don't accept your apologies.
I'm tired of hearing you say that you're sorry.

B MODELS (Read, Discuss and Perform the following model dialogues)

1 *A Woman bumps into another woman while getting off a bus.*
   W1: Oh, excuse me. I'm sorry. That was clumsy of me.
   W2: No need to apologize. These buses are always coming to a sudden stop. I understand.

2 *A man and woman are talking on the telephone.*
   M: June, I really want to apologize to you.
   W: What for?
   M: I'm really sorry about what I said to you the other night.
   W: Oh, forget it.
   M: I can't. It was a terrible thing to say. Please forgive me.
   W: O.K. O.K. Enough is enough. I accept your apologies.

3 *Two musicians are talking just before a rehearsal.*
   M1: Hey, sorry to be late, guys.
   M2: What happened to you last night? You didn't show up.
   M1: Oh, yeah. Sorry about that, too. I just got into something, and I forgot about the time . . .

M2: I don't believe you're sorry. And I don't believe your excuse either. You're out of the group, man.

M1: C'mon, Jake, let's forget about it just this once . . .

M2: Hey, man, it's been more than this once. It's over for you. Get your stuff, and get out.

M1: Hey, I apologize, man.

M2: I don't want no apologies. You're finished . . .

C SUGGESTED ACTIVITIES (Discuss and Perform)

What would you probably do if you were in the following situations?

1 You see someone who looks like a friend. You go up and begin talking. When she turns around, you see it isn't who you thought it was.

2 You're talking with a friend. You make a humorous comment about his clothes, but he doesn't think it's funny.

3 You're talking with a colleague at the office, and accidently knock over your cup of coffee on his/her desk.

10 Wishing Good Luck / Good Fortune

A EXAMPLES (Read, Discuss and Practice)

Good luck.
Best of luck.
I wish you luck.
Good fortune be with you.
I hope that everything goes O.K. for you.
I'm sure that everything will work out just fine.
May you be happy and successful in your new life.

B MODELS (Read, Discuss and Perform the following model dialogues)

1 Two secretaries begin talking.
S1: Well, here goes . . .
S2: Where are you going?
S1: I'm going in to ask Mr. Ladd for a raise.
S2: You're finally going to do it, huh? Good luck. I hope it goes O.K.
S1: So do I.

2 A student is talking with one of his teachers.
T: So, John, have you decided what to do after you graduate?
S: Yeah. I got a job as an assistant in a law office.
T: You did? Well, congratulations. I think you'll do very well. I wish you luck.
S: Thank you very much, sir.

3 An office-clerk is talking with her boss.
OC: Well, Mr. Johnson, I'm leaving now. I just came to say goodbye for the last time.
B: Well, Cynthia, I'm sorry to see you leave. You've been a very good worker. It seems like all the best people get married and leave. Well, may you be happy in your new life . . .
OC: Thank you so much, Mr. Johnson. And good luck to you, too.
B: Thank You, Cynthia.

C SUGGESTED ACTIVITIES (Discuss and Perform)

If you were in the following situations, what would you do?

1 One of your friends is going for a job interview. You meet him/her in the street on the way there.

2 Two people are talking in an office. One has just been transferred to a different city. This is the last time you will see each other.
3 You are talking with an acquaintance at a party. She tells you that she's going to get married soon.

Everyday Functions 2

CHAPTER 2

1 Asking About Activity

A EXAMPLES (Read, Discuss and Practice)

What are you doing?
What'cha doin'?
What'cha up to?
What's up?
What's going on here?
What's happening here?
Where are you going?
Where're ya off to?
Where're ya headin'?

How's it going?
How're ya doin'?
Is everything O.K.?
It goin' O.K.?
You doin' all right?

B MODELS (Read, Discuss and Perform the following model dialogues)

1 *A man sees his neighbor working on his car.*
   M: Hey, Ted, what'ch up to?
   N: I was having a little car trouble this week, so I'm trying to find out what the problem is.
   M: Oh, yeah? How's it going?
   N: Well, not so good. I think it's a bigger problem than I can handle . . .

2 *A friend calls another friend on the telephone.*
   F1: Hello, Chris? This is Leslie.
   F2: Oh, Hi, Leslie. How are you?
   F1: O.K. Listen, are you doing anything right now?
   F2: No. Nothing in particular. Why? What's up?
   F1: I need some help with something . . .

3 *A waitress stops at a table where a man and his wife are eating. She speaks to the man.*
  W: Well, How's it going? Is everything O.K.?
  M: Yes. Everything is fine, thank you.
  W: Oh, Miss, can I have another glass of water, please?
  W: Oh, sure. I'll bring you one in just a few minutes.

4 *A boy sees a friend riding his bicycle.*
  B: Hey! Danny! What's up? Where're ya off to?
  F: I'm on my way to the hobby shop. I gotta pick up some paint for my model airplane. Wanna come?
  B: Sure. Wait up. Let me get my bike . . .

C SUGGESTED ACTIVITIES (Discuss and Perform)

What would you do in the following situations?

1 You want to go to the movies, and you call a friend on the telephone. He says he's busy. You want to know what he's doing.
2 You're taking a walk in the park. You see an acquaintance sitting on a bench making something with an old newspaper.
3 An office manager returns from lunch and finds three of his staff members decorating his office with party decorations.

2 Asking About Trouble / Problems

A EXAMPLES (Read, Discuss and Practice)

Asking about People

What's the matter?
What's wrong?
What's happened to you?
Are you O.K.?
Is anything wrong?
Is there something the matter?
Is everything all-right?

Asking about Machines

Is this toaster broken?
Doesn't this copy machine work?
Is this toilet out of order?
What's the matter with this TV?
What's wrong with this typewriter?
What happened to this hair dryer?

B MODELS (Read, Discuss and Perform the following model dialogues)

1 *Two friends are talking while shopping.*
   F1: . . . and, on our way home, why don't we stop in at Herby's for an ice cream . . . Mary? What's the matter? You look like you've seen a ghost. Mary, are you O.K.?
   F2: Huh? Yeah . . . I'm O.K.
   F1: What happened?
   F2: Alice, did you see that man who just passed us?
   F1: No. I didn't really notice him. Why?
   F2: He looked exactly like a friend of mine who died recently . . .

2 *A wife and husband begin talking.*
   W: Are you still working on the car hon?
   H: *(Unhappily)* Ah, yeah.
   W: You sound pretty depressed. What's wrong?
   H: I think we're going to have to get another car. I don't think I can fix it this time . . .
   W: Oh, no. What's the matter with it?
   H: I think the whole engine needs to be rebuilt.

3 *Two office-workers are talking in the office.*
   OW1: Hey, Jim. Com'ere a minute, will you?
   OW2: Sure. Is there something the matter?
   OW1: Is this coffee machine broken or something?
   OW2: Here, let me see . . . It doesn't seem to work, does it.
   OW1: No. I guess we're goin' to need to get a new one . . .
   OW2: Yeah. Let's put an 'out of order' sign on it . . .

C SUGGESTED ACTIVITIES (Discuss and Perform)

How might the following situations be handled?

1 Two college students are in their apartment. One comes out of the bathroom and sees the other crying in the living-room.

2 Two clerks are trying to use the office copy machine. One tries to make a copy, but no copy comes out of the machine.

3 A man sees his neighbor kicking his power lawnmower.

3 Asking about Thoughts / Feelings

A EXAMPLES (Read, Discuss and Practice)

What are you thinking about?
A penny for your thoughts.
What's on your mind?
You have something on your mind?
What are you looking so serious about?
You seem a little preoccupied about something . . .
Is something bothering you?
Is there anything you want to talk about?
Want to talk about it?

How's it going?
Are you O.K.?
How do you feel about it?
Are you worried about something?
You seem to be in good spirits.
You look a little depressed about something . . .

You sound as if something wonderful just happened.
You seem like you woke up on the wrong side of the bed.

B MODELS (Read, Discuss and Perform the following model dialogues)

1   *A young man and woman are out on a date.*
    W: . . . and I told Mary I thought she made the right decision.
    M: That's interesting . . .
    W: Do you think she did?
    M: Huh? Do I think she did what?
    W: Mike, are you listening to me? Is something the matter?
    M: I'm sorry. It's nothing.
    W: You seem a little preoccupied. What are you thinking about?
    M: Oh, it's nothing important. Really.
    W: Oh, really. C'mon. You can tell me. A penny for your thoughts.
    M: I was just thinking about us going to see my parents . . .
    W: Are you worried about it?
    M: No. Not really worried . . .
    W: Really? Then, how do you feel about it?
    M: I'm just wondering what my parent's reaction will be . . .
    W: You are worried about it, aren't you?
    M: Uhmmm . . . I've told you before . . . They're a little strange . . .

2   *A wife and husband are talking at lunch on Saturday.*
    W: Excuse me asking, but, are you feeling O.K., Jim?
    H: Yeah. I'm O.K. Why do you ask?
    W: You sound a little unhappy about something . . . and you don't sound like your usually happy self either.
    H: Well, to tell the truth, I am a little . . .
    W: A little what? What's the matter?

27

H: Oh, it's just that I'm beginning to hate my job. All I do is work. Here it is, Saturday, and I have to work all day at home. I have no time for you or the kids . . .

W: Well, if you don't like it, why don't you quit?

H: I've been thinking about that . . . How would you feel about it?

W: If it would make you happy, it would make me happy. I wouldn't mind going back to work, either.

H: If you want to, that's fine with me, you know . . .

C SUGGESTED ACTIVITIES (Discuss and Perform)

What would you probably do in the following situations?

1 An elderly man and woman are sitting together on a park bench talking about old times. The man begins to say something, but stops again and again.
2 You are talking with a neighbor. He/she seems a little angry about something.
3 One of your colleagues in your office seems really depressed about something.

4 Asking about Health / Physical State

A EXAMPLES (Read, Discuss and Practice)

How are you?
How're you doin'?
How have you been?
How do you feel lately?
How've you been feeling?
How's your health?
Have you been in good health?
You seem to be in good health.
You're looking healthy.
You look great.
You look as healthy as ever.

Do you feel all right?
Are you feeling O.K.?
You doin' O.K.?
Are you all right?
You sure you're O.K.?
You don't look so good.
You're looking a little pale.
Does something hurt?
Are you in pain?
What hurts?
Where does it hurt?

B MODELS (Read, Discuss and Perform the following model dialogues)

1 *Two friends meet on the street.*
   F1: Hey! Phil! How're ya doin?
   F2: Pretty good, thanks. How've you been lately? Gotten over that cold yet?
   F1: Nah, not yet. It's still with me. You're looking as healthy as ever. How do you do it?
   F2: Thanks. I just take very good care of myself, that's all. Have you been to see a doctor about your cold?
   F1: No. I just can't seem to find the time . . .

2 *Two factory workers begin talking.*
   FW1: *(Coming to her friend)* Mary? Are you feeling O.K.?
   W2: Yeah. I'm O.K.
   FW1: You don't look so good. Your face is a little flushed . . . and you're sweating. Are you sure you feel O.K.?
   FW2: Well, it is a little hot in here, isnt' it?
   FW1: No. I'm quite comfortable. Here, let me feel your forehead. Mary! You're burning up! O.K. Let's go see Mr. Olsen. Let's get you home or to a doctor.
   FW2: No, no, I'll be O.K. in a little while . . .
   FW1: No way. C'mon, let's go . . .

3 *Two friends are hiking together in the country.*
   F1: This is really a beautiful hike, isn't it?
   F2: *(in a tired voice)* Yeah. It's great.
   F1: Are you doing O.K.?
   F2: Yeah. I'm O.K. I'm getting a little tired, that's all.
   F1: Why are you walking like that? Something hurt?

F2: I think I'm getting a little blister. It's nothing.
F1: Do you think you can make it to the lake?
F2: Yeah. I'll make it. Or I'll die trying . . .

C SUGGESTED ACTIVITIES (Discuss and Perform)

Think about how you might handle the following situations.

1   You meet a former neighbor on the street. He/she used to be sick a lot. He/she doesn't look so well now either.
2   A father and daughter are jogging together. The daughter is getting tired and is falling back.
3   You're visiting an old uncle. He's in great health, but he is also a kind of hypochondriac.

5 Asking to be Quiet

A EXAMPLES (Read, Discuss and Practice)

Shhhh!
Please be quiet.
Quiet, please.
Please stop talking.
Would you please not talk.
Could you please hold the noise down.
Would you please give me your attention a minute.
*Shut up!
*Hold your tongue!
*Shush!

B MODELS (Read, Discuss and Perform the following model dialogues)

1 *A group of people are at a surprise party.*
P1: O.K. everyone. He's here. He just parked the car.
P2: O.K. He's coming up the front walk . . .
P1: Now, everyone be quiet . . . shhhh . . .
(The man walks in the door.)
Everybody: SURPRISE!!!

2 *A man is at the theater. Two people are talking behind him.*
P1: . . . do you like her hair like that?
P1: If you ask me, it really doesn't suit her very much . . .
P1: I don't like it either. I think it looks terrible.
P2: I agree with you.

31

M: *(Turning around)* Excuse me, but I'm trying to watch the play. Would you please not talk.

P2: Oh, We're sorry. We didn't think we were bothering you . . .

3 *A little boy is at the supermarket with his mother.*

B: Mommy . . . Mommy . . . can I have some candy.

M: No. Candy's no good for you. You know that.

B: Mommy . . . c'mon. I'm hungry.

M: No. Be quiet, and stop pestering me.

B: How about this one here . . . this little one . . .

M: No. Put that back! And don't ask me again.

B: Mommy. I want some candy . . .

M: Tommy! Shut up. I said no, and that's final.

C SUGGESTED ACTIVITIES (Discuss and Perform)

How would you handle the following situations?

1 You and a friend are out driving. You're listening to the news on the radio. Your friend is talking. An important story comes on.
2 Two college students are at the library. One is serious about studying, but the other wants to talk about an upcoming party.
3 You're at work. You're trying to proof-read a report, but one of your colleagues is singing to himself beside you.

6 Asking to Wait / Not to Wait

A EXAMPLES (Read, Discuss and Practice)

Just a minute.
Wait a minute, O.K.
Can you wait a minute?
I'll be with you in a minute.
Would you mind waiting a moment?
*Hold your horses.
*Not so fast.
Hang on.
Hold on a minute.
Could you please hold?

Wait up!
Wait for me!
Don't go off without me.
Go on without me.
No need to wait for me.
Don't bother waiting for me.

B MODELS (Read, Discuss and Perform the following model dialogues)

1 *A wife asks her husband for help in the kitchen.*
   W: Walter, can you come here and help me with something?
   H: O.K. Can you wait a minute, though? I'll be right there.
   W: O.K. But come as soon as possible . . .

2 *A woman enters the doctor's office and talks with the receptionist.*
   R: Can I help you?
   W: Yes. I have a 2 p.m. appointment with Dr Smith . . . The name is Johnstone.
   R: Yes, here it is. Would you mind waiting a moment? The doctor will see you in a few minutes. Have a seat, please.
   W: Yes, thank you.

3 *Two people are talking on the telephone.*
   P1: . . . so I told Mike to take it back to where he bought it . . . Oh . . . there's someone at the door . . . Hang on a minute, will you? I'll be right back.
   P2: O.K. I'll hang on . . .

4 *A woman is calling the local Chamber of Commerce. A receptionist answers.*
   R: Good afternoon, Martinstown Chamber of Commerce. Could you please hold a moment?
   W: Yes.
   (A few minutes later)
   R: Thank you for holding. How can I help you?
   W: I'd like to speak to Mr Thompson, please . . .

5 *A colleague comes into the office where two people are working.*
   P1: Hey! You guys still working? It's almost lunch-time. You still want to go to Luigi's for lunch with us?

P2: Yeah, I do, but I got a few more things to finish up. Don't bother waiting for me. I'll meet you there.
P1: How about you, Bob?
P2: Yeah, wait up for me. I'll be with you in half a minute.
P1: O.K. We'll save you a seat, then, Frank.
P2: Yeah. Thanks. See you later.

C SUGGESTED ACTIVITIES (Discuss and Perform)

How might you handle the following situations?

1 You and a friend are at the museum. Your friend wants to go home, but you want to continue looking around a little longer.
2 You've got a bad cold, and you call the doctor. The receptionist wants to put you on hold.
3 A boy and girl are going to a party. They get out of the car, and the boy begins walking ahead of the girl.

7 Asking to Postpone

A EXAMPLES (Read, Discuss and Practice)

How about some other time.
Maybe some other time.
Can we wait on that?
Can I have a raincheck on that?
I'll get back to you later on that.
How about we put that off to some other time.
Would you mind if we postponed talking about that until some other time?
*Not now!
*Later, O.K.?

B MODELS (Read, Discuss and Perform the following model dialogues)

1 *A man is talking with a neighbor in his backyard.*
   M: By the way, Phil, do you have any plans for this evening?
   N: Yes, we do. Why do you ask?
   M: Wanda and I were going to invite you and Luanda over for some drinks after dinner
   . . .
   N: Sure . . . How about some other time?
   M: Yeah, O.K. Maybe next weekend or so . . .

2 *A woman is talking with a man who works in the same office.*
   W: Hi, Mark. How's it going?
   M: Oh, Hi, June. Not bad. How about you?
   W: Pretty good. Listen, are you busy tonight? A friend just gave me two free tickets to a movie tonight . . .
   M: I'm sorry, June, but I have plans for this evening. Can I have a raincheck on that? I'd really like to . . .
   W: Oh, sure. Let's make it some other time.

3 *Two businessmen are discussing some contracts.*
   BM 1: . . . O.K. One other thing we have to talk about is the new parts-supply contract.
   BM 2: Uhm, yeah . . . Listen, would you mind if we put that off to another time? We're currently working on our parts-supply systems, and we'll be finished by next week.
   BM 1: O.K. Sure. Let's talk about it next week, then.

C SUGGESTED ACTIVITIES (Discuss and Perform)

If you were in the following situations, what would you do?

1 You work in an office, and have a meeting with another person. But, you have a bad headache. The meeting is not very important.

2 You are shopping and meet an acquaintance. While you're talking, he/she invites you for a cup of coffee at a coffee shop. You have to meet a friend in a few minutes.

3 A friend invites you to an art exhibition at a local museum that evening. You already have other plans.

8 Asking to Think about/Decide

A EXAMPLES (Read, Discuss and Practice)

Asking to Think About
Think about it.
Think it over.
Give it some thought.
Consider it a while.
Please give it your consideration.
I'd like to ask you to consider working with us.

Asking to Decide
Make up your mind.
Decide what you want to do.
Make a decision one way or the other.
Have you made up your mind yet?
So what do you say?
What have you decided to do?
What's your decision?

B MODELS (Read, Discuss and Perform the following model dialogues)

1 *A manager is talking with an employee.*
  M: Excuse me, Mike. Can I talk with you a minute?
  E: Sure. What can I do for you?
  M: I'm working on this year's vacation schedule. Have you thought about when you want to go on vacation?
  E: Uhmmm . . . Not yet. I've been too busy.
  M: Well, you're doing great work, but you need some time off. Think about it, O.K.? Let me know by Friday.
  E: O.K. I'll give it some thought . . .

2 *An insurance agent is talking with a customer on the phone.*
  IA: . . . so, if you're tired of paying so much for car insurance, I'd like you to consider Safe-Life Insurance. I'm sure we can save you money. What do you say?
  C: Uhm, well, I'll think it over . . .
  IA: Yes, please do give it your consideration. Remember, you can never have too much insurance in this uncertain world . . .

3 *Two friends are shopping together.*
  F1: Tell me, Doug. Which pair do you like better?
  F2: I told you . . . I think both pairs are nice.
  F1: I just can't decide which to buy . . .
  F2: C'mon. Make up your mind, will you? It's getting late . . .

C SUGGESTED ACTIVITIES (Discuss and Perform)

What would you do in the following situations?

1 You are talking with a friend. You want to use your camera. He/she seems interested, but can't decide.
2 You are a sales person, and you sell cosmetics door to door. You're talking with a customer who seems to be interested.
3 Two friends are in an ice-cream shop. It is their turn to order. One can't decide what kind of ice-cream to get.

9 Inviting to Join an Activity

A EXAMPLES (Read, Discuss and Practice)

C'mon.
C'mon and join us.
You want to come along with us?
How about going with us?
You're invited to sing, too, if you want.
We'd really like for you to take part in our little show.
Would you like to join us?
Would you be interested in seeing it with us?
Would you care to join our little group?

B MODELS (Read, Discuss and Perform the following model dialogues)

1 *Two room-mates are talking as one is leaving the apartment.*
   RM 1: I'll see you later, O.K.?
   RM 2: Where're ya off to?
   RM 1: Marty and Phil are going shopping . . . to Northgate Mall. Oh, you want to come with us?
   RM 2: Yeah . . . No, maybe not. I'd better finish working on this report for Econ. class . .
   .

2 *Two friends are talking at a party.*
   F1: This has been a pretty nice party, hasn't it.
   F2: Yeah, it has been. Listen, a group of us are going out for a few more drinks afterwards. Would you be interested in going too?
   F1: Yeah. That sounds good. Where are you going?

3 *Two office-workers meet at the coffee machine during break-time.*
   OW 1: Hey, Martha . . .
   OW 2: Yeah?
   OW 1: A group of us are going to go to the *Music in the Park* series this lunch time. How about coming with us?
   OW: 2 That's a great idea. I've been wanting to go to one . . .

C SUGGESTED ACTIVITIES (Discuss and Perform)

How might the following situations be handled?

1 You are leaving English class with some friends to go to a coffee shop. You meet an acquaintance coming from the other direction. He/she is alone.
2 A college student is studying in the library with a friend. He wants to take a break and go for a walk. He invites his friend.
3 You're at a party and you're going to go out dancing afterwards with some friends. You want to invite a person, whom you're very interested in, to go with you.

10 Telling to Hurry / Not to Hurry

A EXAMPLES (Read, Discuss and Practice)

Telling to Hurry
Hurry! Hurry up!
Quickly!
Can you please rush this?
Would you mind working a little faster?
*Move it!
*Be quick about it!
*Let's get moving!
*Get a move on it!
*What are you waiting for?
*What's keeping you?

Telling not to Hurry
Slow down.
Don't hurry.
Don't rush.
Take your time.
Take it easy.
Do it slowly and carefully.
Let's not rush things.
Don't be in such a hurry.
No need to hurry.

B MODELS (Read, Discuss and Perform the following model dialogues)

1 Two friends are going to go to a movie.
F1: Hey, Fred. It's 6.30 p.m. The movie starts at 7.00. Hurry up, will you. Let's go.
F2: O.K. Hang on a minute. I'll be ready in two minutes.
F1: O.K., but be quick about it. I hate being late for a movie.

2 A store manager is talking with a new cash-register clerk.
SM: How's it going, Marty?
CC: O.K. I'm getting used to the cash register, watch me
SM: Let's see. O.K. O.K. Take it easy. Slow down. Remember, accuracy is more important than speed.

3 A mother is taking her daughter to the orthodontist.
M: Mary! Get a move on it! We're almost late for your appointment.
D: Here I am. I'm ready. By the way, Mom, can I go out tonight?
M: Go out? Where? With whom?
D: Uhm . . . Out with Larry Holmes . . . to a beach party . . .
M: What? No, you may not. You're only 15 years old, young lady. Let's not rush things. You have plenty of time to . . .
D: Aw, Mom. Everyone else is going . . .

C SUGGESTED ACTIVITIES (Discuss and Perform)

What would you do if you were in the following situations?

1 A mother and son are shopping. The mother is anxious to go home. The son wants to go to the sporting-goods shop.
2 A father and son are working on the family car together. The son wants to work quickly and go for a drive. The father wants to do a careful job.
3 You're going to a party, and your room-mate is taking a long long time to get ready.

11 Telling to Be Calm / not to Worry

A EXAMPLES (Read, Discuss and Practice)

Calm down.
Take it easy.
Stay calm.
Keep cool.
Be patient.
Hold on to yourself.
Dont't get in an uproar.
Don't let things get to you.
Don't be upset.

Don't worry.
You don't have to worry.
Don't take things so seriously.
Don't let it bother you.
Don't sweat it.
There's no need to worry.
Worrying isn't going to do any good.

B MODELS (Read, Discuss and Perform the following model dialogues)

1 *A man is talking with a friend after pulling him from a fight.*
   M: C'mon, Flip, Calm down. Keep cool.
   F: You heard what he called my brother, didn't you?
   M: It's O.K. Don't let it get to you.
   F: I don't have to take that from him. I'll . . .
   M: C'mon, Flip. Take it easy, will you . . .

2 *A man and woman are sitting at a table in a restaurant.*
   M: . . . Where is that waiter? What's keeping him?
   W: It's O.K., John. Be paitient. We have time.
   M: But this place is almost empty. There's no excuse for us to wait this long . . .
   W: I know, dear. But don't let it get to you. Remember your blood pressure . . .

3 *A secretary is talking with another secretary.*
   S1: Oh, Judy, I think I lost the Harrison report . . .
   S2: Don't worry about it. It'll turn up.
   S1: I can't imagine where I put it.
   S2: Does anyone need it right now?
   S1: No. Not right now . . .
   S2: O.K. Take it easy. Maybe you'll remember where you put it . . .

C SUGGESTED ACTIVITIES (Discuss and Perform)

Think about how you might handle the following situations.

1 You and a friend are out for a drive. You come upon an accident. Your friend becomes hysterical. You want to help the people in the accident.
2 An office manager is talking with a new secretary. It is her first day, and she has made many mistakes. She is upset.
3 It is 2 a.m., and a teen-age boy's parents are waiting for him to come home from a party.

12 Telling to Go First

A EXAMPLES (Read, Discuss and Practice)

Go on.
Go ahead.
You first.

You may go first.
Ladies first.
Ladies before gentlemen.

B MODELS (Read, Discuss and Perform the following model dialogues)

1 *A man and woman bump into each other while entering a shop.*
   M: Oh, excuse me. I'm sorry.
   W: Oh, that's O.K. We both seem to be in a hurry.
   M: That's true. *(Opening the door)* Here. You first.
   W: Thank you.

2 *Two friends are waiting for an elevator.*
   F1: Oh, here's the elevator. Go on, you first.
   F2: No. You go ahead.
   F1: No. You may go first.
   F2: Oh, all right. If you insist.
   F1: Thank you.

3 *An elderly man and woman are going to a restaurant for lunch.*
   M: Here we are, my dear.
   W: Why, thank you, Henry. This is such a nice idea . . .
   M: *(Opening the door)* Ladies first.
   W: Oh, Henry. You're always such a gentleman . . .

C SUGGESTED ACTIVITIES (Discuss and Perform)

How would you probably handle the following situations?

1 You're getting on a bus. The pregnant woman beside you wants to get on too.
2 A man and woman are talking with the host at a party. The host asks a question, and they both answer at the same time.
3 You're on your way to class with your teacher. You reach the door to the class-room first.

13 Telling Not to Interrupt / Not to Disturb

A EXAMPLES (Read, Discuss and Practice)

Telling not to Interrupt

Hold on a minute.
Please don't interrupt.
Could you please wait a minute.
Could you please not interrupt.
*Not now.
*Don't interrupt me.
*Stop interrupting me.
*Can't you see I'm on the phone?

Telling not to Disturb

Please don't disturb me.
If you don't mind, I'm a little busy . . .
I'm sorry, but I'm busy.
*Stop bothering me.
*Don't pester me.
*Get lost.
*Buzz off.
*Get away from me.
*Leave me alone, will you.
*Don't be such a nuisance.

B MODELS (Read, Discuss and Perform the following model dialogues)

1 *A father is on the telephone and his son runs up to him.*
   F: . . .and I also want to order item 028 – 47D . . . That's the . . .
   S: Daddy, Mommy wants you . . .
   F: Timmy, please don't interrupt. I'm on the telephone.
   S: Daddy, Mommy says . . .
   F: Timmy, not now. Can't you see I'm talking on the phone.
   S: Daddy, Mary hurt herself. Mommy says come quickly.
   F: What! O.K. Tell Mommy I'll be right there. (*Speaking into the phone*) I'm sorry, an emergency came up. I'll call again later . . .

2 A beggar comes up to a young tough on the street.
  B: Excuse me, sir, but could you help a poor man who . . .
  YT: Hey, man, don't bother me.
  B: But, as you can see, sir, I haven't . . .
  YT: Hey, listen, buzz off, will you.
  B: Yes sir. I was just about to leave . . .

3 An artist is finishing a painting. A friend comes in.
  F: Hey, Roberto. Did you see this article in the paper?
  A: Uh, no.
  F: It says the mayor is expected to sign the new anti-discrimination ordinance soon . . .
  A: Steve . . . please don't bother me right now, O.K.? I really need to concentrate on this. . .
  F: Oh, O.K. Sorry. I'll talk to you about it later . . .

C SUGGESTED ACTIVITIES (Discuss and Perform)

Suppose you were in the following situations. What might you do?

1 A husband and wife are talking about household finances. Their 6-year-old son comes in and asks for something to eat.
2 A TV repairman is trying to fix a big, complicated TV set. A friend comes in and wants to ask him something.
3 You're watching an important film on TV. Your little brother or sister comes in and wants you to play a game.

14 Telling to be Serious / Not to Lie

A EXAMPLES (Read, Discuss and Practice)

Telling to be Serious
C'mon.
Be Serious.
Are you serious?
You're pulling my leg.
*Get out of here.
Are you kidding?
You must be joking.
That's not funny.
Cut the comedy.
Knock off the jokes.

Telling not to Lie
Please tell the truth.
*You don't expect me to believe that, do you?
*What do you take me for? A fool?
*What kind of fool do you think I am?
*Don't lie to me.
*Nonsense!
*Bull!
*Your full of it.
*That's a crock!

B MODELS (Read, Discuss and Perform the following model dialogues)

1 *A wife and husband are discussing vacation plans during lunch.*
H: Well, hon, any ideas about where to go for our vacation?
W: How about Brazil? We've both always wanted to go . . .
H: Are you kidding? Where'll we get that kind of money?
W: I'm serious. I got a bonus today. $5000.
H: What? Aw, c'mon. You're pulling my leg.
W: No, I'm not. Mr. Haber has been so impressed with my work that he decided to give me a big bonus . . .

2 *Two college students are talking in the library.*
CS 1: Hey, Jim. You know that girl you were interested in?
CS 1: You mean Laura? What about her?
CS 1: I hear she's beginning to get interested in you, too.
CS 1: Really? Aw, c'mon. Knock it off. That's not funny . . .
CS 1: I'm not kidding. I heard it from Jennifer.
CS 1: Huh? Oh, bull! You don't expect me to believe that, do you?
CS 1: I swear it's the truth. Jennifer was talking to her . . .

3 *A lawyer is talking with a client in jail.*
L: O.K., Harry, now tell me where you really were the night that Marcy Hopkins was killed.
C: I told you. I was in a bar. The Stork Club. With some friends of mine.
L: C'mon, Harry. Don't lie to me. I know you weren't there.
C: Yes, I was. You can ask Joe, the bartender . . .
L: Harry, what kind of fool do you take me for? I did check with Joe. I pressured him a little, and he told the truth . . .

C SUGGESTED ACTIVITIES (Discuss and Perform)

What would you probably do in the following situations?

1 You are shopping, and you meet an old friend. He says he's going to get married soon. You think he's joking.
2 A son comes home at 3 a.m. from a date. He tells his mother he had a flat tire. She doesn't believe him.
3 A teacher is asking a student who always turns in things late for his term paper. The student begins to make up a story.

15 Telling to Begin / Stop Doing Something

A EXAMPLES (Read, Discuss and Practice)

Get going!

Get started now!

Let's get crackin'.

Get moving on this right away!

Get on this immediately!

Why don't we begin.

How about we get started on that report.

What do you say we begin cleaning up the yard.

*Stop it!

*Quit it!

*Lay off!

*Cut it out!

*Knock it off!

Knock off the noise!

Would you mind not humming.

Will you please stop typing.

Could you please not play your radio so loud.

B MODELS (Read, Discuss and Perform the following model dialogues)

1 *An office manager is talking with some staff members.*

OM: . . . O.K., everyone. Now that we all know how important this project is, let's give it our best. What do you say?

SM 1: O.K. with me.

SM 2: You can count on me.

OM: O.K. Well, let's get started on it right now, then.

2 *A mother is talking with her daughter.*

M: Frieda, have you begun cleaning up your room yet?

D: Uh, no, not yet, Mom.

M: Well, what are you waiting for. Get crackin'. I want it clean by the time your father gets home.

3 *Two people are working in the same small office.*

P1: Hey, Jane, Knock it off, will you?

P2: Knock off what?

P1: Would you mind not tapping your pencil on the desk. It's driving me crazy.

P2: Oh, I'm sorry. I didn't notice I was doing it. Take it easy, huh? Is there something the matter?

C SUGGESTED ACTIVITIES (Discuss and Perform)

How might the following situations be handled?

1 Two college students are going to have a party at their apartment. One tells the other to begin cleaning up.
2 You are talking with a friend at lunch. He/she is complaining about his/her job. You're getting tired of listening.
3 Your son or daughter keeps banging pots and pans together in the kitchen. You are getting a headache.

16 Showing an Unwillingness to Continue

A EXAMPLES (Read, Discuss and Practice)

I give up.
I've had it.
The hell with it.
I'm throwing in the towel.
I can't handle this anymore.
This is a waste of time.
It's not worth the effort.
It's hopeless.

There's no more I can do.
What's the use of trying?
It's useless trying to talk with you.
I'm sick of hearing your complaints.
I'm fed up with your excuses.
I've had enough of this place.
I'm full up to here with his bragging about his success.

B MODELS (Read, Discuss and Perform the following model dialogues)

1 *A wife comes into the kitchen and finds her husband working.*
   W: Harold, what are you working on there?
   H: I'm trying to fix this old clock . . .
   W: What's wrong with it?
   H: It's always slow. I've been working on it for an hour now, but can't seem to get it . . . Oh, hell, I've had it. It's not worth the effort. Let's throw it out.
   W: Fine with me. I've been wanting a new one . . .

2 *Two college room-mates are talking.*
   RM 1: Marty, will you please stop putting your feet on the table.
   RM 2: Oh, don't worry about it. It's old.
   RM 1: Yeah, but who always ends up cleaning it? Me!
   RM 2: Well, then, don't clean it. It doesn't bother me . . .
   RM 1: But it bothers me.
   RM 2: Why?
   RM 1: Oh, I give up. It's useless trying to talk with you . . .

3 *Two office workers are talking during their lunch break.*
   OW 1: Are you still thinking of seeing Tom again sometime?
   OW 2: Oh, no. I've had enough of him. He keeps calling me on the phone, but I hang up on him now.
   OW 1: Oh, really. It's that bad now, huh?
   OW 2: Yeah. I've just decided I couldn't handle it anymore . . .

C SUGGESTED ACTIVITIES (Discuss and Perform)

What would you do in the following situations?

1 You're talking with a friend about a problem. He/she always asks you for advice, but never listens.

2 A man and woman have recently separated. The man wants to continue the relationship, but the woman doesn't.
3 You're playing tennis with a friend, and you have lost fifteen straight games.

17 Showing Excitement/Enthusiasm

A EXAMPLES (Read, Discuss and Practice)

Wow!	I'm glad to hear that.
That's great!	That's a great idea.
Fantastic!	That sounds fantastic.
Super!	What a fantastic idea!
Oh, boy!	How wonderful!
Far out!	Count me in.
That's wonderful!	I'll buy that.
All right!	I'm with you all the way.
Yeah!	

B MODELS (Read, Discuss and Perform the following model dialogues)

1 *Three college students are talking in a coffee shop.*
   CS 1: Hey, Mike, what's that you're reading?
   CS 2: It's a letter from a company I applied for a job with. They're offering me a job after I graduate.
   CS 3: Wow! That's fantastic!
   CS 1: Yeah. That's great. Congratulations.
   CS 2: Thanks, guys.

2 *A father, mother and son are talking at Friday dinner.*
   M: Well, it's Friday. What shall we plan on doing tomorrow?
   F: Oh, how about going to the zoo. Would you like that, Billy?
   S: Oh, boy! Super! Can we really go?
   F: I don't see why not . . . unless it rains. How about it, Mary?
   M: It sounds like a good idea to me.

3 *Three office workers are talking during their morning break.*
   OW 1: . . . well, what do you say we go out for lunch together . . . the three of us?
   OW 2: That's a good idea.
   OW 3: Count me in. Where should we go?
   OW 1: I was thinking of the Club 84. I'll treat you . . .

C SUGGESTED ACTIVITIES (Discuss and Perform)

Think about how you might handle the following situations.

1 You call a friend on the phone. He mentions that he recently won a lot of money in a lottery.
2 A man is talking with his boss. The boss says the company will sponsor a bowling team. Bowling is the man's favorite sport.
3 A girl tells her friends that her family has decided not to move to a different part of the country after all.

18 Showing Indifference/Resignation

A EXAMPLES (Read, Discuss and Practice)

So what?
Who cares?
I don't care.
What does it matter?
What difference does it make?
Who gives a damn?
The hell with it.
I couldn't care less.

Big deal.
Do what you want.
Anything's O.K. with me.
It's all the same to me.
What can I do?
Why bother?
What's the use?
It's not worth the effort.

B MODELS (Read, Discuss and Perform the following model dialogues)

1 *Two women are talking during lunch at a restaurant.*
   W1: Oh, by the way, I heard something about your ex-husband the other day . . .
   W2: About Jack? Who cares?
   W1: He's apparently going out with a 21-year old college girl now.
   W2: To tell you the truth, I couldn't care less. What he does is his business.

2 *Two teachers are talking about the school where they work.*
   T1: . . . Barry, have you heard the latest news? It appears that we won't be laid off after all.
   T2: Oh, so what. I'm fed up with working here anyway.
   T1: We also might be getting a $100 a month raise.
   T2: What difference does it make? We'll still be earning peanuts.
   T1: Wow. You're in a pretty bad mood, aren't you . . .

3 *Two students are talking on their way to class.*
   S1: Hey, Bob! Are you going to join the protest march today?
   S2: Oh, why bother. Nothing's going to change from it.
   S1: You never know. The administration might listen to us this time . . .
   S2: Not a chance. Do what you want, but don't include me . . .

C SUGGESTED ACTIVITIES (Discuss and Perform)

What would you probably do in the following situations?

1 You are talking with a friend. He/she mentions that an old boy/girlfriend of yours has just gotten married.
2 Two office workers are talking. One was expecting a promotion but didn't get it. He/she wants to show indifference.
3 A student has just found out that he failed a course. He didn't go to class very often and didn't do any of the work.

51

19 Showing a Strong Negative Reaction

A EXAMPLES (Read, Discuss and Practice)

You're crazy!
Are you crazy?
You're nuts!
That's insane.
Have you gone bananas?
You're out of your tree!
You're out of your mind!

You're off your rocker.
What's the matter with you?
Are you feeling O.K.?
have you been out in the sun too long?
Where are your brains?
You got rocks in your head!

B MODELS (Read, Discuss and Perform the following model dialogues)

1 *Two friends are talking on the telephone.*
   F1: . . .so, what are you planning to do this weekend?
   F2: I was thinking of driving down to the shore . . .
   F1: Are you crazy? It's Labor Day week-end. The traffic will be murder.
   F2: Yeah, well, I know some good back roads that are never busy . . .

2 *An 8-month pregnant woman is talking with her husband.*
   W: Mike . . . You know what I feel like doing?
   H: No. What's that?
   W: I feel like going horseback riding?
   H: Are you out of your mind? In your condition? Horseback riding?
   W: I know it's a crazy idea, but I really feel like doing it. I'll be O.K.
   H: You're nuts. Wait until after the baby comes.
   W: Oh, c'mon hon. I'll be really careful . . .

3 *Two office managers are talking about a new project.*
   OM 1: Sally, should we talk to Leslie about our ideas for this new project?
   OM 2: What's the matter with you. He'll steal our ideas.
   OM 1: Then what do you think we should do?
   OM 2: Let's not talk to anyone until the project meeting . . .

C SUGGESTED ACTIVITIES (Discuss and Perform)

Suppose you were in the following situations. What would you do?

1 You are talking with a friend. She's talking about a first date she had the night before, and says she's going to get married.

2 Two office workers are talking about money problems. One says he's going to ask the boss for a raise. Both know that everyone who has asked for a raise has been fired.

3 Your brother, who has just bought his first motorcycle the day before, tells you he's going to enter a dangerous motor-cycle race in two weeks.

20 Showing a Limit of Knowledge

A EXAMPLES (Read, Discuss and Practice)

I don't know.
I don't think I know.
I'm sure I wouldn't know.
Beats me.
You got me there.
Who knows?
God only knows.

I have no idea.
That's beyond me.
That's a new one on me.
How am I supposed to know?
Why are you asking me that?

B MODELS (Read, Discuss and Perform the following model dialogues)

1 *Two college students are talking on a Sunday afternoon.*
   CS 1: Mark. Do you know where I can get a bottle of Scotch today?
   CS 2: Hmmm. Beats me. The liquor stores are closed on Sundays.
   CS 1: The supermarkets don't carry liquor, do they?
   CS 2: Are you kidding? Of course not. Not in this state.

2 *A wife asks her husband something.*
   W: Harry, do you know how the blender works?
   H: How am I supposed to know? Why? Is there something wrong with it?
   W: Yeah. It's making a strange noise when I turn it on . . .

3 *Two factory workers are discussing a new company policy.*
   FW 1: Marty, when does the new 15-minute limit on breaks start?
   FW 2: I don't know.
   FW 1: Why are they doing it? It seems like a strange idea.
   FW 2: God only knows why they're doing it. If you ask me, it's a stupid policy.

C SUGGESTED ACTIVITIES (Discuss and Perform)

1 A husband and wife are talking about a friend who recently committed suicide. They can't understand it.
2 You are talking with a friend who wants to buy a piano.
3 A woman is asking her boyfriend about his ex-wife. He has had no contact with her for a long time.

Requests and Offers 3

CHAPTER 3

1 Help / Assistance

A EXAMPLES (Read, Discuss and Practice)

Requesting Help/Assistance
Help!
Help me!
Got a minute?
Can you give me some help with this?
I could use some help with this.
Could you give me a hand?
Would you mind helping me a minute?
Could you open the door for me?

Offering Help/Assistance
Can I help you?
Need some help?
Can I give you a hand?
Need a hand?
Let me help you with that.
I'll help you with that.
Could you use some help?
Can I be of assistance?
Is there anything you need help with?
If you need help with anything, please let me know.

B MODELS (Read, Discuss and Perform the following model dialogues)

1 *A mother and daughter are doing laundry in the laundromat.*
   M: We're finally finished. Oh, here comes Mrs. Sweeny. She's got a bundle there. Go and offer to help her . . .

D: O.K. Mom. Hi, Mrs. Sweeny. Would you like some help?

W: No, no. I can carry it. But, could you hold the door open for me? I can't get it.

D: Sure. Is this O.K.?

W: Yes. That's just fine. Thank you for your help.

2 *A man is looking for something in a department store. He is approached by an assistant.*

A: Can I help you, Sir? Is there anything in particular that you're looking for?

M: No, thank you. I'm just looking.

A: O.K. Take your time. If you need help, let me know.
(Later)

M: Excuse me, can you help me with something?

A: Yes, Sir. What is it you're looking for?

M: I'm interested in this gold pen and pencil set . . .

3 *A man and woman watch a boy fixing a flat tyre on a car.*

W: That boy looks like he can use some help with that tyre.

M: Oh, he's doing O.K.
(After they walk past.)

B: Help me! Somebody help me!

W: Look, John, the car fell on that boy's foot!

M: Yeah. I'd better help him . . . Here, son, let me help you with that. Does your foot hurt?

B: Yeah . . . It's on my toes . . . Please try and hurry . . .

M: O.K. O.K. Take it easy. Stay calm.

C SUGGESTED ACTIVITIES (Discuss and Perform)

1 You are bending over to pick up a handkerchief you dropped. Your back goes out of joint. You can't stand up.
2 A factory worker is trying to move a large, heavy box. She is having a hard time. She asks a fellow worker for help.
3 You see a young man looking at a map of the city where you live. He seems lost. You offer to help.

2 Favors

A EXAMPLES (Read, Discuss and Practice)

Asking for a favor
Do something for me, will you?
Take care of this for me, please.
Can you do me a favor?
Do me a favor, will you?
May I ask you for a favor?
Would you mind doing me a favor?
Can you take care of this for me?
Would you mind writing this letter for me?

Offering a favor
Here, let me read that for you.
I'll do that for you.
I'll take care of it for you?
Shall I call him for you?
Is there anything I can do for you?
Let me know if there's anything I can do for you.

B MODELS (Read, Discuss and Perform the following model dialogues)

1 *A husband and wife are at home with their baby.*
   H: Are you changing her diaper again?
   W: Yeah. (*Hearing the oven alarm*) Oh, what's that. I have to take the pie out of the oven . . .
   H: Do you want me to take it out? Or, shall I change the baby?
   W: Can you finish doing the baby? I'll take care of the pie.
   H: Sure. C'mon, little girl . . . Let's see that diaper . . .

2 *Two friends are talking at home.*
   F1: . . . by the way, Chris, can you do me a favor?
   F2: Sure. What is it?
   F1: I have to call the travel agency about Jim's flight to Las Vegas. I don't think I have time. Would you mind?
   F2: No, not at all. What agency is it?
   F1: Thanks. It's Tour-All Travel . . .

3 *A man and woman are working in an office.*
   M: I can't believe it. I was sick one day, and I come back to all these papers on my desk.
   W: Yeah, it looks pretty bad. Is there anything I can do?
   M: Can I ask you for a small favor? I have to proof-read these reports by noon, and I don't think I'll get them all done . . .
   W: O.K. Let me have a couple. I'll do them for you.
   M: Oh, and do one other thing for me, will you?
   W: O.K.
   M: Could you drop this off at Tom's office? If I do, he'll want to talk as usual, and I don't have time today . . .
   W: Oh, yeah, I know what he's like. Sure, I'll drop it off . . .

C SUGGESTED ACTIVITIES (Discuss and Perform)

What would you probably do in the following situations?

1 You are at the library with a friend and want to take out a book. You have forgotten your library card.
2 You are driving home from work in the rain and you see a colleague walking without an umbrella.
3 Your mother has a bad headache, but has to go shopping for food for dinner. You offer to go for her.

3 Permission

A EXAMPLES (Read, Discuss and Practice)

Asking for Permission

Can I close the window?
Please let me have the car tonight.
May I close the window?
Do you mind if I smoke?
Is it O.K. if I use your typewriter?
Would you mind if I went with her?
Permit me to borrow your pen a minute.
May I have your permission to marry your daughter?

Giving Permission

Sure, go ahead.
It's O.K. with me.
Fine with me.
No, I don't mind.
Why not?
You have my permission.
I won't stop you.

Denying Permission

No, you may not.
You can not.
Yes, I do mind.
I don't think so.
You do not have my permission.
I will not permit you to.
I absolutely forbid you.

B MODELS (Read, Discuss and Perform the following model dialogues)

1 *A boy is asking his mother for permission to go to the movies.*
   B: Mom, can I go to the movies with Tim and the guys tonight?
   M: No, you may not. You've been to two movies this week.
   B: Please. Mom. Please let me go. Tonight's the last night . . . I'll do anything you want me to . . .
   M: Will you clean the garage this afternoon before you go?
   B: Uhmmm . . . O.K. How about half today and half tommorow?
   M: O.K. It's a deal. You can go.

2 *A man is visiting an acquaintance's home for the first time.*
   M: This is really a nice apartment you have.
   A: Thank you. I felt lucky to find it.
   M: By the way, do you mind if I smoke?
   A: No, I don't. Go ahead. I'll get an ashtray for you.

3 *Two strangers are sitting next to each other on a bus.*
   S1: Excuse me, but I'm a little warm. Is it O.K. if I open the window?
   S2: Fine with me. I'm a little warm also.
   S1: Thanks. Ah, that's better.

C SUGGESTED ACTIVITIES (Discuss and Perform)

How might the following situations be handled?

1 You are a friend's house. The window beside you is open and you feel cold.
2 A student has to type a paper for class the next day, but his typewriter is broken. His room-mate's is in good condition.
3 You're at work, and you want to ask your boss if you can have tomorrow off.

4 Promises

A EXAMPLES (Read, Discuss and Practice)

Asking for a Promise
Promise me that you'll write once a week.
Do you promise to take care of the dog if we get one?
Make me a promise, will you?
I want you to promise that you'll love me forever.
Is that a promise?'
Cross your heart and hope to die?
Do you give me your word on that?
Do you swear that you won't forget me on Mother's Day?

Offering a Promise
I promise I'll buy you one.
I promise you that I'll be home by 12 p.m.
I promise to drive you to school tomorrow morning.
I'll make you a promise I'll never see him again.
It's a promise.
I give you my word on that.
You have my word on it.
I swear that I'll pick up your suit on the way home.

B MODELS (Read, Discuss and Perform the following model dialogues)

1 A son is asking his mother for permission to watch TV.
  S: Mom, can I watch TV? *Superman* is on now.
  M: Have you finished your homework yet?

S: No, but I'll finish it after. I don't have very much.
M: Do you promise to start it as soon as the program is over?
S: Yeah. I promise.
M: What do you promise?
S: I promise I'll do my homework as soon as the program is over.
M: O.K. Go ahead. You can watch it.

2 *Two women meet by accident in a jewelry store.*
   W1: Why, Cathy! I haven't seen you in a long time.
   W2: Francine! Imagine meeting you here. How long has it been?
   W1: It's been quite a while, hasn't it. I'm sorry, Joan, I'd love to talk, but I'm late for a lunch meeting . . .
   W2: O.K. But let's try to get together sometime soon . . .
   W1: O.K. I'll call you tomorrow . . .
   W2: Is that a promise?
   W1: It's a promise. Talk with you tomorrow, O.K.?
   W2: O.K. Take care.

3 *Two businessmen are talking about a sales agreement.*
   BM 1: How can I be sure that the materials we need will get here on time?
   BM 2: They will. You have my word on it.
   BM 1: Well, O.K. You've been dependable in the past, so I guess we can rely on that dependability this time.
   BM 2: Don't worry. I swear to you the materials you need will be on time.

C SUGGESTED ACTIVITIES (Discuss and Perform)

How would you handle the following situations?

1 A friend of yours is visiting your home. She sees some books she wants to read. She has borrowed books in the past, and hasn't returned some of them.
2 Two college room-mates have graduated and are going their separate ways. They want to make sure they keep in contact.
3 A son is asking his very busy father to promise to play tennis with him during the week-end.

5 Congratulations

A EXAMPLES (Read, Discuss and Practice)

Congratulations!
Congratulations on your new baby.
Let me congratulate you on your new job.
Let me say congratulations on winning the first prize in the tournament.
I'd like to say congratulations. You did a great job.

B MODELS (Read, Discuss and Perform the following model dialogues)

1 *Two college students are talking on the telephone.*
   CS 1: Hey, I forgot to ask you the last time I called did you ever hear about your scholarship?
   CS 2: Oh, yeah. Haven't I told you? I got it.
   CS 1: Really? That's great news. Congratulations!
   CS 2: Thanks a lot, Cindy. Yeah, I'm really happy . . .

2 *Two office workers begin talking.*
   OW 1: Hey, Vic, I heard your wife had a baby the other day.
   OW 2: That's right. A little girl.
   OW 1: Well, let me say congratulations. What's her name?
   OW 2: We named her Hester, after my mother . . .

3 *A professional golfer is being awarded a prize by the president of a sponsoring corporation.*
   M: . . . well, Larry, you've done it. You've won the Grand Desert Classic. I'd like to say congratulations. How does it feel?
   PG: It feels great. Thank you.
   M: And here, with your prize money, is Mr. John Carter, President of the Dunlop Corporation, sponsors of the tournament.
   P: Thank you, Mr. Rossi. Congratulations on winning the tournament, Larry.
   PG: Thank you very much, sir.
   P: And, now, on behalf of the Dunlop Corporation, I would like to present you with a check for $150 000 . . .

C SUGGESTED ACTIVITIES (Discuss and Perform)

If you were in the following situations, what would you do?

1 You meet a friend at the drug store. While talking, she mentions that she has found a new job.
2 You are talking with an acquaintance at a party. He is an author. He says he has just sold his latest book.
3 The daughter of your next-door neighbor has just finished medical school. You see her for the first time since she finished.

6 Compliments

A EXAMPLES (Read, Discuss and Practice)

Offering Compliments

Your apartment *is fantastic.*
I like your new hairdo.
You certainly have good taste in clothes.
That's a nice pair of earrings you have on.
I thought you handled that situation *really well.*
What a beatiful garden!
How nice you look tonight!
I must compliment you on your tennis game. You played well.
My compliments to you on this delicious meal.
May I compliment you on your choice of a wife.
I'd like to compliment you on your report.

Accepting a Compliment

Thank you.
Oh, it was nothing.
Do you think so?
Oh, they're really not very good.
Thank you for the compliment.
I appreciate the compliment.
Flattery will get you nowhere.
You're just flattering me.

Rejecting a Compliment

Don't give me that.
Don't try and flatter me.
I don't like flatterers.
You're just flattering me.
Flattery will get you nowhere.
Nonsense.
You're full of baloney.

B MODELS (Read, Discuss and Perform the following model dialogues)

1 *A man and woman are at a restaurant on their first date.*
   W: That's a really nice tie you have on tonight. I like it.
   M: Thank you. I think you look really nice tonight, too.
   W: Do you think so? This is wonderful place. How did you ever find it?
   M: A friend recommended it. I've been here a couple of times before. It has a nice atmosphere.
   W: I agree. I must compliment you on your good taste . . .

2 *A young man is talking with the clerk at a driving center.*
   C: Can I help you, Sir?
   YM: Yes. I want to get a driver's license.
   C: O.K. Fill out this form and bring it back to me here.
   YM: Yes, Ma'am. *(Later)* Here it is, Ma'am.
   C: O.K. Let me see . . . O.K. Everything looks fine . . .
   YM: Wow! You have really nice handwriting . . .
   C: Don't try to flatter me, young man. Flattery will get you nowhere.
   YM: I'm not trying to flatter you. I honestly think it's nice . . .

3 Two businessmen are talking after a meeting.

BM 1: I thought you did a great job in the meeting just now, John. Your report was very well-done.

BM 2: Thanks a lot. I was pretty nervous, though.

BM 1: I know. But you handled the situation really well. My compliments to you.

BM 2: Well, I tried to do my best . . .

C SUGGESTED ACTIVITIES (Discuss and Perform)

How would you probably handle the following situations?

1 You are at a party. A friend has just finished singing a song.
2 A husband and wife are playing golf together. The wife hits a long-iron shot that lands two feet from the pin.
3 You are going out for dinner with a friend. He/she is very dressed up and looks very nice.

7 Praise / Credit

A EXAMPLES (Read, Discuss and Practice)

Offering Praise/Credit

Nice work, Alice.

Nice going, Bob.

You did a great job, Manuel.

That was *a great* game, Ali.

You deserve a lot of credit for all the work you've done, Lucy.

I have to give you credit, Fred. That was a masterstroke.

I'd like to give credit to Tina Jones for the beautiful cake.

I've got to hand it to you, Toshi. You did very well.

I want to acknowledge Linda's contributions to this bazaar's success.

Requesting Praise/Credit

Don't I get any credit?

Don't I deserve some credit for what I did?

What credit do I get for helping you all these years?

You have to give me some credit too, you know.

Wasn't what I did worth anything?

What about my contributions?

B MODELS (Read, Discuss and Perform the following model dialogues)

1 *A group of friends are drinking after a volley-ball game.*

F1: Hey, guys, can you believe it? We actually won!

F2: Yeah. And against the best team in the league. Tony, you played a great game tonight.

F3: Yeah, Tony. We have to give you credit. You won it!

F1: O.K. O.K., guys. Enough is enough. Cheers!

F2: Here, here!

2 *Some business-people are talking after a project meeting.*

BP 1: Maxine, you deserve a lot of credit for all you've done to make this project a success.

BP 2: I'll say. You did a great job.

BP 3: Thank you, but I can't take all the credit. You guys did most of the work . . .

BP 1: Yeah, but you organized us . . .

3 *A young husband and wife visit the wife's mother and father.*

F: My goodness, Martha, isn't little Gertie beautiful?

M: What a gorgeous baby! She must have gotten all her good looks from you, Les.

H: Do you think she really looks like me? She really is beautiful, though, isn't she . . .?

W: Wait a minute, everyone . . . Don't I get any credit for having this beautiful baby?

F: Of course, Sue. We were only teasing you . . .

C SUGGESTED ACTIVITIES (Discuss and Perform)

What would you say in the following situations?

1 A teacher and student are talking. They are discussing a term paper the student wrote. The teacher gave it an A + .
2 You are talking with a friend who recently rescued some people from a house fire.
3 You work in an office, and you and a colleague recently redecorated it. The boss has come in and is thanking you. Your colleague is taking all the credit, but it was your idea and you did most of the work.

8 Encouragement/Discouraging

A EXAMPLES (Read, Discuss and Practice)

C'mon,
Go on!
Hang in there!
Go, man, go!
Keep it up!
Don't give up!
Keep your chin up!
Don't get discouraged!
Keep up the good work!
Keep on pushing!
You're doin' great!
Keep the faith!
I want to encourage you to try out for the team.
Let me encourage you to keep on studying in school.

Give up!
Don't bother with it.
Don't waste your time.
It's not worth the effort.
What do you want to do that for?
You don't really want to do that, do you?
You really want to do that?
That's a lousy plan if lever heard one.
I don't want to discourage you, but you'll never make it.
I don't mean to put you down, but that won't work.

B MODELS (Read, Discuss and Perform the following model dialogues)

1 *A student is talking with her advisor about quitting school.*
   S: I don't know, Mr. Gamon. I'm getting kind of discouraged. I'm about to give up . . .
   A: Is that so. Already. How long has it been?
   S: Two quarters, so far.
   A: You're doin' O.K. for your second quarter. Stick with it. Keep your chin up! Don't let yourself get discouraged. And have patience with yourself. Things take time . . .
   S: Yeah, I guess. Thanks for the pep-talk, Mr. Gamon . . .

2 *A son is talking with his father after dinner.*
   S: Dad, I want to try out for the football team.

F: Now, what do you want to do that for? You'll just get hurt.
S: Gee. Thanks for the encouragement, Dad.
F: Aw, c'mon, son. You know I want the best for you . . .

3 *Some business-people are talking during breaktime.*
   BP 1: . . . I think that that's a really good idea, Joan. I want to encourage you to bring it up at the management meeting next week.
   BP 2: Do you really think it's a good idea?
   BP 1: It's a great idea.
   BP 2: What do you think, Sally?
   BP 3: Well, I'd say don't waste your time. It's a good idea, but management will never go for it . . .

C SUGGESTED ACTIVITIES (Discuss and Perform)

What could you do in the following situations?

1 You are a teacher, and one of your best students feels bad because he/she recently did poorly on a test.
2 You are the father/mother of a teen-age boy. He wants to quit high school and find a job.
3 Two factory workers are having lunch together. One of them is having a hard time learning a new job.

9 Sympathy/No Sympathy

A EXAMPLES (Read, Discuss and Practice)

Offering Sympathy

That's too bad.
That's a shame.
What a pity!
Tough break.
Better luck next time.
What a terrible thing to have
happened.
I'm sorry to hear that.
It must be pretty rough on you.
I can imagine you feel bad.
I sympathize with you.
I know how you must feel.
I know what you mean.

Showing no Sympathy

That's too bad.
That's a shame.
What a pity!
Tough luck.
Tough break.
I'm really sorry to hear about that.
That's the way it goes.
That's life.
That's the way the cookie crumbles.
You got what you deserved.
I have no sympathy for you.

Accepting Sympathy

Thank you.
That's very kind of you.
It is a pity, isn't it?
Oh, well, such is life.
So it goes, I guess.
Better luck next time.

Rejecting Sympathy

Don't feel sorry for me.
You don't need to feel sorry for me.
Don't give me your sympathy.
Oh, leave me alone.
I don't want your pity.
I don't need your sympathy.

B MODELS (Read, Discuss and Perform the following model dialogues)

1 *A woman is talking with a friend in a small restaurant.*
   W: What's the matter, Doris? Have you been crying?
   F: Oh, Joe and I just split up.
   W: No. Really? I'm sorry to hear that.
   F: He said he was tired of my always criticizing him. He said he didn't want to hear anymore.
   W: I know how you must feel. I was shaken when Bob and I broke up.
   F: I hate men. Why do they always do this to us?

2 *Two office workers are talking at lunch.*
   OW 1: How did your racquetball game go this morning?
   OW 2: I lost. 21 to 9 and 21 to 14.
   OW 1: That's too bad. Better luck next time. Who did you play?
   OW 2: Malcolm. What's more, I broke a tooth while playing.
   OW 1: Let me see . . . That looks like it hurts. Does it?
   OW 2: Not as much as before . . .

3 Two students are talking after their chemistry class.
- **S1:** So, Stu, how did you do in the Chem. exam?
- **S2:** Don't ask. I failed it.
- **S1:** Oh, that's too bad. Well, you got what you deserved, didn't you. You didn't study at all, did you.
- **S2:** Oh, shut up. I'm not interested in talking about it.
- **S1:** Well, maybe next time you won't give me such a hard time about studying all the time . . .

C SUGGESTED ACTIVITIES (Discuss and Perform)

What would you probably do in the following situations?

1 You are talking with a friend. There was a fire in his apartment building. He lost a lot of his things.
2 A friend calls you on the phone. He invested a lot of money in a phony oil company and lost all of it. You advised him not to invest in it, but he ignored your advice. Now he wants to borrow some money.
3 A colleague of yours at your office has just told you that his/her pet dog was hit by a car and killed last night.

10 Condolences

A EXAMPLES (Read, Discuss and Practice)

Offering Condolences

I'm sorry.

I'm sorry to hear about your father.

I'm sorry to hear that your little Tweetie died.

Let me offer my condolences.

Let me tell you how sorry I am to hear about your grandmother.

I know how you must feel . . .

It must be pretty hard on you . . .

You must feel terrible about losing your brother like this . . .

Responding to Condolences

Thank you.

That's very kind of you.

There's nothing that can be done about it.

It's God's will, I suppose . . .

God giveth and God taketh away . . .

B MODELS (Read, Discuss and Perform the following model dialogues)

1 *A man meets a friend after his father's funeral.*
   F: Mike. How are you?
   M: Fine, thanks. And you?
   F: O.K. I'm sorry to hear about your father. It must be pretty hard on you.
   M: Yeah, it is. We were pretty close. It's harder on my mother, though.
   F: I can imagine.

2 *Two neighbors begin talking in their backyards.*
   N1: Mary. What's the latest news on your brother?
   N2: He had his operation the other day, but the doctors say the cancer is too far advanced . . .
   N1: I'm sorry to hear that.
   N2: Yeah, well, there's nothing we can do. It's God's will.

3 *A friend is talking with a deceased person's sister at the funeral services.*
   F: Good afternoon, Grace.
   S: Martin. I'm so glad you could come.
   F: I'm very sorry to hear about your brother's death. It must be pretty hard on you . . .
   S: It is. He was so young. Why did he have to die?
   F: I know how you must feel. I felt like Gunther was my brother too . . .
   S: Well, God giveth and God taketh away . . .

C SUGGESTED ACTIVITIES (Discuss and Perform)

If you were in the following situations, what would you do?

1 A friend of yours recently lost a brother in a motor-cycle accident. You meet her by chance in the supermarket.
2 Your best friend's dog just died. He loved the dog deeply. You go to visit him in his home.
3 You are attending an acquaintance's mother's funeral ceremony. You just arrive, and meet him/her just inside the door.

That's a fascinating painting, don't you think?

Direct
Functions 4

CHAPTER 4

1 Agreeing / Disagreeing / Refusing

A EXAMPLES (Read, Discuss and Practice)

Asking for Agreement

That's a nice looking boat, huh?
He's a lousy player, isn't he?
That's a fascinating painting, don't you think?
We'd better finish this today, don't you agree?
He's not to be trusted Isn't that so?
Don't you agree that this plan is too risky?
Are you in agreement with us?
Do you agree to help us if we need help?
Would you go along with a 2% membership fees increase?
Do we have a deal?

Agreeing

I agree.
I know what you mean.
I think so, too.
That's for sure.
Right on.
Certainly.
O.K. with me.
Fine with me.
I agree to do so.
I'll go along with that.
It's a deal.

Disagreeing /Refusing

I don't agree.
I disagree.
I don't think so.
I'm not so sure.
I find I can't agree with you.
I can't agree to that.
I can't go along with you on that.
I refuse.
No way.
No deal.

B MODELS (Read, Discuss and Perform the following model dialogues)

1 A group of business-men are discussing a decision.

BM 1: Well, gentlemen, I think this is the best choice we have . . .

BM 2: I agree. It seems a good choice.

BM 3: Well, I'm not so sure about it. There are a few things I think we've overlooked . . .

2 A club president is asking for the members' agreement to a plan.

CP: Well, everyone, do we all agree that the charity bazaar is our highest priority project this month?

M1: I think so.

M2: I agree.

CP: And do all of us agree to contribute one night a week to work on it?

M3: I agree to.

M2: Fine with me.

CP: How about you, Fred?

M4: I'm sorry, but I can't go along with you on that. I'm working two jobs now . . .

3 A lawyer and his client are talking about his divorce.

L: O.K., Jim. It seems as if your wife's going to ask for half of everything: half the property, half the investments, etc. Do you agree to that?

C: O.K. I agree.

L: And she wants custody of the children.

C: I'm not sure I agree. What visiting privileges do I get?

L: She said any time any week-end.

C: Well, I guess I'll go along with that.

L: And, lastly, she wants the dogs.

C: What? No way! I refuse. That's where I draw the line . . .

L: She says that the dogs belong with the kids . . .

C SUGGESTED ACTIVITIES (Discuss and Perform)

How might the following situations be handled?

1 You are talking with some friends about friendship. You want to see if other people agree with your views.
2 You and one of your fellow office workers are talking about working conditions. You disagree with some things he/she says.
3 A teen-age boy wants to use the family car. He is asking his father for permission. His father puts some conditions on using the car. The boy agrees to some, disagrees to others.

2 Supporting / Opposing / Objecting To

A EXAMPLES (Read, Discuss and Practice)

Asking about Support/Opposition/Objections
Do you support the President's new foreign policy?
Are you in favor of this proposal?
Are you for equal rights for women?
Who supports this idea?
Who favors changing the club's rules?
Does anyone support Mr. Johnson's idea?
Is anyone in favor of taking a five-minute break?
Do you oppose this plan?
Are you opposed to sending the army there?
Do you object to my running for treasurer?
Do you have any objections to postponing the meeting?
Who is not in favor of this suggestion?
Would anyone have any objections to adjourning until after lunch?
Can I have your support?
Can I count on your support?
Will you support me in my campaign for governor?

Supporting
I'll support Mr. Thomas.
I'm in favor of equal rights.
I'm in total support of it.
I'm for postponing it.
I have no objection to changing the rule.
You have my support.
I'll give you my support.
You can count on me.

Opposing/Objecting to
I oppose that.
I'm in opposition to this plan.
I'm against cutting the budget.
I object.
I object to the language.
I have an objection.
I cannot support you.
I shall oppose him.

B MODELS (Read, Discuss and Perform the following model dialogues)

1 *Two businessmen are talking before a meeting.*
  BM 1: Listen, Harry, can I ask you a question? Are you in favor of this new training program?
  BM 2: Yes, I am. I've been working on it, so I'm in full support of it. Aren't you?
  BM 1: I basically support it, but I want to suggest a change. Can I count on your support?
  BM 2: That depends on what the change is.
  BM 1: O.K. Briefly, it's as follows: I think we should . . .

2 *A group of people are talking during a cocktail party.*
    P1: . . . Does anyone support the President's tax-cut program?
    P2: Well, I oppose it. I think it will cause too many problems.
    P3: I object to the timing of it. It's too little too late.
    P4: Well, I'm for it. It's the best alternative we have . . .
    P1: That's two against, and one for. As for me, I'm against it too. I don't think it will help
    the country . . .

3 *A club chairperson is leading a members' discussion on a proposal.*
    C: . . . We have a proposal to sponsor a marathon to raise money for the Children's
    Hospital. Are there any objections?
    M1: Yes, I object. I think it's a good idea, but I don't think very many people will par-
    ticipate in it . . .
    M2: I agree with Mildred . . .

C SUGGESTED ACTIVITIES (Discuss and Perform)

How would you handle the following situations?

1 You are a member of an outdoor club, and another member comes and asks your support for a proposal for a two-day hike.
2 Two people are talking in the company cafeteria about the company plan to change to
a four-day work week. One is in favor of it and the other seems to be against it.
3 You want to run for president of your English class. You want to get support from
other class-mates.

3 Announcing

A EXAMPLES (Read, Discuss and Practice)

Attention, please.
Please give me your attention.
Can I have your attention, please.
I have an announcement to make.
I'd like to make an announcement.
Here is an announcement from the Secretary of State's Office.
I'd like to announce that our recruitment drive is a success!

B MODELS (Read, Discuss and Perform the following model dialogues)

1 An announcer comes on the public address system at an airport.

A: Attention, please. Attention, please. Will United Airlines passenger William James on Flight 287 to Miami please report to the United Airlines ticket counter. Passenger William James please report to the United Airlines ticket counter. Thank you.

2 An M.C. is going to announce the winner of a beauty contest.

M.C.: Excuse me, everyone. Can I have your attention, please. I have an announcement to make. The judges have finished their balloting in the Miss Orange County Beauty Pageant, and I would like to announce the winner at this time. The new Miss Orange County is . . . Miss Frieda Harshbaum. Let's all give her a big round of applause . . .

3 A group of people are at a party. A woman calls for attention.

W: Excuse me, can I have everyone's attention. I'd like to make an announcement. I'd like to announce that our dear friends, Lester Randolph and Patty Marshall, are going to be getting married . . .

C SUGGESTED ACTIVITIES (Discuss and Perform)

If you were in the following situations, what would you do?

1 You are the manager of a city bus station. People are waiting for a bus, and you just found out the bus will be late.
2 You are a member of a community action group on housing. The group is having a meeting, and you were just talking with a TV reporter who wants to do a news presentation on the group. You want to tell the other members.
3 You are at a party, and a friend has just told you he/she has just won a big lottery. You want to tell the other people at the party!

79

4 Ordering

A EXAMPLES (Read, Discuss and Practice)

Give me that!
Be quiet!
Don't sit there!
Do this right now, will you!
Stop it, I tell you!
Will you hurry up!
I order you to get out!

Will you please stop talking!
Would you please stand up!
Could you please give me that!
Do you mind not smoking!
Would you mind waiting here!

B MODELS (Read, Discuss and Perform the following model dialogues)

1 *A family, mother, father and son, are visiting the Zoo.*
  M: I'm glad we came here today. The kids seem to be enjoying themselves a lot . . .
  F: I am too. Aren't you . . . Where's Jimmy going? Come here! Don't go so close to that cage!
  M: Come over here, will you, Jimmy!
  S: Aw, Mom, it's O.K. I just want to see better.
  F: The sign says not to go near the cage. Come here, I tell you.
  S: Aw, Dad . . .

2 *Two factory workers are on the assembly line.*
  FW 1: Tom, would you mind not humming!
  FW 2: Oh, is it bothering you? I'm sorry.
  FW 1: I'm sorry, too. I have kind of a bad headache today.
  FW 2: Take some aspirin. I have some. You want two tablets?
  FW 1: Uhmmm, That's probably a good idea . . .

3 Two hunters are having an argument with a farmer.
F: Hey, you two. I order you to get off this property!
H1: *(To the other hunter)* Who's this guy?
H2: I don't know. *(To the farmer)* What do you want?
F: I want you to get off this property!
H1: And who are you to tell us to get off it?
F: I'm the farmer who owns this land. You didn't ask me for permission, so I'm ordering you off my property.

C SUGGESTED ACTIVITIES (Discuss and Perform)

If you were in the following situations, what would you do?

1 A young boy is taking a nap in his bedroom. His mother comes in and sees the dirty, messy room. She becomes angry and wakes him up.
2 A high-school teacher comes into the class-room and finds all the students playing and fighting.
3 You are a 5-year-old boy and your big sister has just taken your bicycle.

5 Urging

A EXAMPLES (Read, Discuss and Practice)

C'mon, Jack, look inside.
Go on, open your present.
Go ahead, Bill, ask her!
Give it a try!
Try it!
Try talking with him one more time.
Why don't you offer to help her?
I want to urge you to vote for me on Primary Day, next Tuesday.
Let me urge you to consider our new economy-sized models.

B MODELS (Read, Discuss and Perform the following model dialogues)

1 *Two friends are talking at an ice-cream shop.*
   F1: Here. You want to try some of my almond peppermint?
   F2: No. I'll stick to my vanilla.
   F1: Aw, C'mon. Try some. You can't eat just plain vanilla ice cream all your life. Try something new. Here . . .
   F2: O.K., but just a little. *(Tasting it)* Uhm . . . it's O.K., but nothing special . . .
   F1: Oh, you're hopeless . . .

2 *A mother is talking with her teen-age son in the kitchen.*
   M: Your father's out in the garage cleaning it up. Why don't you go out and offer to help him.
   TS: Aw, Mom, I'm a little tired right now. Maybe later.
   M: Go on. He'll appreciate the help.
   TS: He's probably finished by now . . .
   M: No, he isn't. He just started. Go ahead. Offer to help.
   TS: Oh, O.K.

3 *A political candidate is answering a man's question.*
   M: Mr Johnson, what can we do if we don't want to pay increased property taxes?
   PC: Well, let me urge you to vote for me. I have long been against raising property taxes as a way to secure city revenue . . .

C SUGGESTED ACTIVITIES (Discuss and Perform)

What would you do in the following situations?

1 You're shopping with a friend who wants to buy a new coat. You see a nice one and want to urge him/her to buy it.

2 Two office workers are at a nice restaurant for lunch. One is urging the other to try some of his/her food.
3 You're a college student, and your room-mate doesn't know whether to accept a job offer or not. You think it's a great opportunity for your room-mate.

6 Scolding / Reprimanding

A EXAMPLES (Read, Discuss and Practice)

Shame on you!
You should be ashamed of yourself.
Aren't you ashamed of yourself?
What a bad little boy you are!
What a terrible thing to say to him!
How rude of you!
You shouldn't have hit your little brother!
How would you feel if someone did that to you?
How would you like it if someone ignored you like that?

B MODELS (Read, Discuss and Perform the following model dialogues)

1 *A little girl comes crying to her father about her brother.*
   F:　Linda, what are you crying about now?
   LG: Tommy hit me.
   F:　Tommy, did you hit your sister?
   B:　No. I didn't hit her.
   LG: Yes, he did. You hit me right here. Look, Daddy . . .
   F:　It looks to me like you hit her. Shame on you, Tommy. Boys shouldn't hit girls. Don't you know better?
   B:　Aw, Dad. She was messin' up my game . . .

2 A teen-age boy and his girlfriend are talking after school.

TB: . . . and so I told him he had breath like a horse . . .

G: You didn't, did you? What a terrible thing to say.

TB: Oh, lay off me, will you. He deserved it. He's been bad-mouthing me for a long time . . .

G: But, still, how would you feel if someone said that to you?

3 Two friends are talking in the office after lunch.

F1: . . . So, how's your diet going?

F2: Well, not so good. I had a big banana split for lunch . . .

F1: What! Aren't you ashamed of yourself? After all the suffering so far, you spoil it with a banana split.

F2: But I just couldn't resist it . . .

C SUGGESTED ACTIVITIES (Discuss and Perform)

How might the following situations be handled?

1 A little girl is playing in the living-room. While she is playing, she knocks over her mother's favorite vase. Her mother hears the noise and comes in.
2 A police officer sees a couple of teenage-boys throwing stones at a small dog in the park.
3 You are at a party, and your room-mate, who has recently quit smoking, is lighting up a cigarette.

7 Warning / Cautioning / Threatening

A EXAMPLES (Read, Discuss and Practice)

Watch out!
Look out!
Heads up!
Be careful!
Don't move!
Halt! Or I'll shoot!
Watch your step with Mr Fulsome.
Be careful with that gun!
Don't you come any closer . . .
Stop that, or else I'll call the police.
You're treadin' on thin ice, Mister.
I'm going to count to 10. 1 . . . 2 . . . 3 . . . 4 . . . .
I'm warning you. If you don't leave me alone, I'll scream
I'm giving you a warning. Get out of town by sunset.
This is my last warning. Stop seeing my wife, or else.
Let me caution you about dealing with the Myrster Company.

B MODELS (Read, Discuss and Perform the following model dialogues)

1 *A husband and wife are walking in the park.*
   H: . . . and why don't we buy Jimmy a camera for his birthday?
   W: That's a good idea. I'm sure he'll like that . . .
   H: Watch out! You almost stepped in that dog-doo there . . .
   W: Whew, that was close, wasn't it. Ah, now, what were we talking about?
   H: Buying Jimmy a camera for his birthday . . .

2 *A bank robber is trapped in the bank by police.*
   P: Come on out, Smith, or we'll come in after you. I'm warning you.
   BR: And I'm warning you, Copper. Don't try and come in. I'll blast anyone who tries to get in here . . .
   P: Don't threaten me, Smith. This is my last warning: If you don't come out right now, we're sending in tear gas . . .

3 *Two businessmen are talking during lunch.*
   BM 1: We're going to need someone to replace Mike Thomas after he retires, you know.
   BM 2: What do you think of Larry Nelson? He's a go-getter.
   BM 1: Hmmm, he's a good choice. But let me warn you, Frank Hardy seems to think he's in line for Thomas's position. He'll probably be very upset . . .
   BM 2: Yeah, I thought about that too. That may be a problem . . .

C SUGGESTED ACTIVITIES (Discuss and Perform)

Think about how you might handle the following situations.

1 You are a teacher. One of your students has missed a lot of classes and a lot of tests. You are talking with him/her in your office.
2 You and a friend are shopping downtown. You're talking, and he/she begins to cross the street without looking.
3 You are walking on a dark, lonely street at night. You are stopped by two muggers. You are a Kung Fu and Karate expert.

8 Illustrating with Examples

A EXAMPLES (Read, Discuss and Practice)

Giving Examples
For example . . .
For instance . . .
Here's an example . . .
Let me give you an example of what I'm talking about.
I can give the following examples . . .
I have two examples I can give . . .
I want to illustrate this point with an example . . .
Another example would be . . .

Asking for Examples
Like what?
For example? For instance?
Can you give me an example?
Can I have an example of behavior showing ethnocentrism?
Do you have an example of poor construction techniques?
I'd like an example of how to use this word.
Is there an example you can give us?

B MODELS (Read, Discuss and Perform the following model dialogues)

1 *A man and woman are talking at a basket-ball game.*
  M: . . . and I think there's lots of things I could do if I quit my job?
  W: For example?
  M: Well, for example, I could get a job with the city government. My managerial experience would help. Another example would be getting a job with one of our competitors . . .

2 *Two students are studying together in their room.*
  S1: . . . Maria, in the book on page 142, it says, "People generally have little awareness of what they communicate non-verbally." Do you understand what that means?
  S2: I think I do.
  S1: Can you give me an example of what they're trying to say?
  S2: Hmmm, let's see. O.K. For instance, a father tells his child that he loves her, but he says it in an angry voice. The father thought he communicated love, but the baby understood anger. The father wasn't aware of the non-verbal content of his message.
  S1: I see. That's a pretty good example . . .

3 A coach is giving a lecture to a sport's club.

    C: . . . and there's a lot you can do to make junior league football safer for your kids. Let me give a couple of examples. One is that you can have regular equipment checks. Before the start of every game, check every player's equipment to make sure they have all the equipment and that it's in good condition. A second example would be that you can modify some of the junior league rules . . .

C SUGGESTED ACTIVITIES (Discuss and Perform)

Think about how you might handle the following situations.

    1 You are talking with a friend about good cold remedies. You give examples of ones that you know.

    2 You and a friend are talking about fear. You are saying that you usually don't feel afraid in situations where other people do. You give some examples.

    3 A teacher is talking about unusual ways to learn English. Students in the class ask for some examples.

9 Defining / Clarifying

A EXAMPLES (Read, Discuss and Practice)

Asking for Definition/Clarification

What does horrendous mean?
What is the meaning of fruity?
What does the expression get lost mean?
Can you define debate?
Please define what nolo means.
What do you mean by that?
What do you mean when you say it's impossible?
Does that mean that you don't want to marry me?
Are you saying that he did it on purpose?
For me, this means that you're not interested in the plan . . .

Defining/Clarifying

Fatigued means tired.
The meaning of amateur is not professional.
The definition of landlord is a person who owns property for rent.
A definition of gallop would be to run with long steps.
Let me define what I mean by barbaric: barbaric means treating other people like a
barbarian . . .
I want to give you a definition of milksop: a milksop is a person with no courage or fighting
spirit.
By bumbler I mean a person who can do nothing right.
What I mean when I say it was a blast *is that* I really enjoyed being there.
That means I won't be able to come tomorrow.
What I mean is that I hate him.
Let me clarify that point. All of us need to think about . . .

B MODELS (Read, Discuss and Perform the following model dialogues)

1 *A student is asking the teacher for a definition of a word.*
   T: . . . and he was regarded by many as a dilettante.
   S: Excuse me, Dr. Larson. What does dilettante mean?
   T: A dilettante is a person who does something but is not really very serious about it.
   S: How do you spell it?
   T: D-I-L-E-T-T-A-N-T-E.

2 *A foreign student asks her room-mate for some help.*
   FS: Mildred, excuse me . . . but in the book here it says, "an incumbent candidate always has an advantage in a political campaign." What is the meaning of incumbent?

RM: Incumbent means in office. An incumbent candidate is the candidate who is in office, as opposed to the candidate who does not have the office but wants it.

3 *A man and woman are talking while shopping.*
   M: How about we stop in at Morky's for lunch . . .
   W: Oh, great!
   M: What do you mean when you say, "Oh, great!"?
   W: What I mean is that we've been there an awful lot lately, haven't we? I know it's cheap, but . . .

4 *A politician is giving a speech to a group of voters.*
   P: . . . and, in the coming years, we're all going to need a lot of gumption. Let me define what I mean by gumption: Gumption is courage, stubbornness, laughing in the face of hard times. The coming years are going to be hard ones. They will test our gumption . . .

C SUGGESTED ACTIVITIES (Discuss and Perform)

If you were in the following situations, what would you do?

1 You are talking with a friend about religion. You are not the same religion, and he uses some words you don't know.
2 You are a college student, and have just gotten a part-time job as a teacher's assistant. The teacher is explaining your responsibilities. There are some things you don't understand.
3 You are reading a textbook, and there are some words you don't understand. You ask your teacher for the meanings.

10 Reporting Other People's Speech / Quoting

A EXAMPLES (Read, Discuss and Practice)

Asking about what people said

What did he say?

What did you say to him?

What was that he asked?

Is that what he really said?

Did he actually say that?

What should I tell Dad?

What do you want me to ask her?

What were his exact words?

Do you remember exactly what he said?

Were those his exact words?

Is that a question?

Are you quoting her?

Indirect Reporting

John said that he'll send it to you next week.

Mr. Jones said to open the package as soon as it arrives.

He told me that he's too busy to come to the meeting.

Dr. Alye told me to watch the operation carefully.

Professor Johnson asked me if I did my homework.

Mary asked where the party was.

According to Bob, the plane is going to be late.

Mr. Winston, you're quoted as saying that democracy is dead.

Tell him that I think he's out of his mind.

Tell all of them to stop making so much noise.

Ask your mother where the can opener is.

Ask Ms. Smy if she knows where the Jones report was filed

Direct Reporting/Quoting

John said, "I'll send it to you next week."

Mr. Thomas asked, "How are we supposed to know that?"

My father asked, "Have you finished your homework yet?"

Mr. Winston, you're quoted as saying, "Democracy is dead."

The chief said, and I quote, "This is a dirty business."

Let me quote John Tyler, who said, "You're never too old to learn something new."

General Reports

People say that he can't be trusted.

I've heard that it's an excellent movie.

I'ts rumored that the company is going bankrupt.

Rumor has it that you're going to be promoted.

Dr. Calron, you've been quoted as saying that you won't meet with the President, even if you're asked. Is that true?

B MODELS (Read, Discuss and Perform the following model dialogues)

1 *Two men are talking during a coffee-break at work.*
   M1: Hey, Les. Congratulations. I hear you're getting a transfer and promotion.
   M2: Not if I can help it.
   M1: You mean, you don't want it?
   M2: That's what I mean.
   M1: Have you told Franklin that yet?
   M2: Yep. I told him I wouldn't accept it.
   M1: What did he say?
   M2: He said, "Think it over for a few days." He also said that if I didn't accept it, I'll never be offered the chance again.

2 *A boy is helping his father in the garage.*
   F: Jeff, go tell your mother we're almost finished, and ask her when lunch will be ready.
   B: *(Going to the kitchen)* Mommy, Daddy says that we're almost finished, and he asked when lunch will be ready.
   M: Tell your father to come in as soon as you're done. It's ready now.
   B: O.K. *(Returning to the garage)* Mommy said to come as soon as we're done because lunch is ready now.

3 *Two women are talking about their fiancees.*
   W1: Did you ask if he wants to go to the opera this Friday?
   W2: Yes, I did.
   W1: What did he say?
   W2: He said, and I quote, "Are you kidding?"
   W1: Is that all he said?
   W2: No. He went on to say that he couldn't understand how anyone could like that garbage.
   W1: What a peasant he is . . .

4 *Two professors meet on their way between classes.*
   P1: Chris! How's it going?
   P2: O.K. for me. How about you?
   P1: Not too bad. Hey, rumor has it that Weston is going to be made head of the department. Is that true?
   P2: I've heard that too. I don't really know. If you ask him, he says he's not interested in it. But what he says and what he does are often very different things.
   P1: Yeah. I know. Well, I've got to run. I'm on my way to class. Say hello to Marty and the kids for me.
   P2: Yeah, sure. Same to Bobby . . .

C SUGGESTED ACTIVITIES (Discuss and Perform)

How might the following situations be handled?

1 You and a fellow worker are talking. He is telling you about a conversation about overtime work he recently had with the boss.
2 A woman is talking with an acquaintance during lunch in a restaurant. She is telling the acquantance about a conversation she recently had with a mutual friend.
3 You're from a foreign country, and you're working as an interpreter for a business-person from your country as he/she talks with an American business-person.

11 Specifying / Generalizing

A EXAMPLES (Read, Discuss and Practice)

Asking for Specification
Specifically . . .?
Can you be more specific?
Can you give a specific case?
Can you give a case in point?
Exactly when will he come?
What exactly do you want?
Can you be more exact?

Specifying
Specifically . . .
To be more specific . . .
Here's a specific case . . .
A case in point would be . . .
To be exact . . .
There are exactly fifteen people in the other room.

Generalizing
People are generallly not to be trusted.
As a general rule, ignore about half of what she says.
In general, you can't expect help from other people.
Generally speaking, the weather here is pretty nice.
In most cases, you're safer not getting out of the car.
They are, on the whole, a very peaceful people.
On the average, it rains twice a week here.
I see an average of twenty people a week in this office.

B MODELS (Read, Discuss and Perform the following model dialogues)

1 *Two college professors are being interviewed by a reporter.*
   R: Drs. Hammond and Nelson, both of you have been teaching for many years now. How do you feel about the preparedness of present-day college students for college study?

P1: I'd say that, in general, students nowadays are just not as well prepared as in the past.

P2: To be specific, I think that reading and writing skills are not as good as those of students in the past. People just cannot read and write very well . . .

P1: And, generally speaking, knowledge of Math and Science is comparatively lacking . . .

2 *A man and woman are having an argument.*

M: . . . and I think women shouldn't try to do men's work.

W: Wait a minute. Specifically, what kind of work can't women do?

M: Well, a case in point would be fishing.

W: And why not?

M: On the average, women are not as strong as men.

W: And how important is strength in fishing?

3 *A sales-person is talking with a customer.*

C: When can we expect delivery of these parts?

SP: As you know, Mr Lawson, we always deliver on time . . .

C: Yes, I know. But this time we need an exact delivery date. If those parts are even one day late, it means trouble for us . . .

C: We'll have them to you next week . . .

C: Can you be more exact?

SP: O.K. I'll have them to you on Wednesday, at the latest . . .

C SUGGESTED ACTIVITIES (Discuss and Perform)

What would you do in the following situations?

1 An office manager is asking a typist when she'll be finished typing a report. She doesn't want to give an exact answer.

2 A talk-show interviewer is asking you questions about your home country.

3 Two people are talking about their philosophy of life and relations with other people.

12 Qualifying

A EXAMPLES (Read, Discuss and Practice)

For me . . .
As I see it . . .
From my point of view . . .
To my mind . . .
Let me qualify that . . .
I'd like to qualify what I said . . .
I want to add the following qualification to what I said . . .

B MODELS (Read, Discuss and Perform the following model dialogues)

1 *Two women are talking at the library.*
   W1: Tracy, have you read this book?
   W2: Let me see . . . Yeah, I read it a couple of years ago.
   W1: How did you like it?
   W2: It was really interesting. At least, for me it was interesting. I'm not guaranteeing you'll like it . . .
   W1: Well, you generally have pretty good taste . . .

2 *Two young people are talking at a convention.*
   P1: That was quite an interesting presentation, wasn't it.
   P2: Did you think so?
   P1: From my perspective it was. I learned quite a few things I didn't know before.
   P2: Is that so? Like what?
   P1: Well, for example, I learned that . . .

3 *The president of a company is speaking to stockholders.*
   P: Excuse me, but I find I must qualify something I said earlier. I said that the dividend will be raised this year. What I should have said is that the dividend will be raised if the government changes its current restrictions on trade with China, which is expected to happen . . .

C SUGGESTED ACTIVITIES (Discuss and Perform)

How would you handle the following situations?

1 A new sales-person is asking an experienced one for a recommendation about a good place to take clients to. The experienced person recommends one, then qualifies it.

2 A friend asks for your opinion of a movie you saw recently. You praise it highly, then qualify your opinion.
3 A TV news reporter asks you about American food. You state your opinion, then begin to qualify it.

Asking About/ Expressing

5

1 Surprise/Amazement

A EXAMPLES (Read, Discuss and Practice)

Expressing Surprise/Amazement

Huh? What?
Oh! Wow!
What a surprise!
What a surprise it is to meet you here!
This is a nice surprise!
I'm surprised at you.
I'm really surprised I can.
Incredible!
That's unbelievable!
Amazing!
I'm amazed at the news.
That was an amazing show.
It was beyond belief!

Asking about Surprise/ Amazement

Are you surprised?
Does that surprise you?
Is this a surprise?
What surprised you?
What's so surprising?
You don't seem so surprised.
Isn't this incredible?
Isn't it amazing?
Aren't you amazed?
Can you believe it?
What's so amazing about that?

B MODELS (Read, Discuss and Perform the following model dialogues)

1 *A group of people are having a surprise party for an actress.*
   P1: O.K. Everyone. Here she comes. She's out of the elevator.
   P2: O.K. Now, everyone be quiet. When she opens the door, we turn on the light and yell "Surprise!" Shhhh.

(The actress opens the door and enters the apartment.)
All: Surprise!!! Happy Birthday!!!
A : What . . . Wow! What a surprise! What is all this?
P3: A birthday party for you, Julia dear. Are you really surprised? You really didn't suspect anything?
A: I'm truly surprised. I didn't have the faintest idea . . .

2 *Two friends are at a gymnastic exhibition.*
   F1: Wow! She's an amazing gymnast!
   F2: I know. Now, watch this next movement . . .
   F1: Huh! That's incredible. I never would have believed anyone could do that . . .
   F2: Yes, she is quite good, isn't she?
   F1: What do you mean, "quite good"? She's beyond belief!

3 *A woman is talking to her husband about their baby.*
   W: Guess what, dear. Megan said her first word today.
   H: Really? What did she say?
   W: You'll never guess. She said "apple juice".
   H: Really. Two words? That's amazing. Were you surprised?
   W: I sure was. What a bright child we have . . .

C SUGGESTED ACTIVITIES (Discuss and Perform)

Suppose you were in the following situations. What do you think you would do and say?

1 You are at a fast-food restaurant, and you hear hear a somewhat familiar face call your name. It's an old friend you haven't seen for ten years.
2 A husband and wife are celebrating their first wedding anniversary. The husband got up early and made breakfast. He also hid a gold bracelet under a roll on the plate. He brings the tray to his wife in bed.
3 It's your English teacher's birthday, and everyone in the class has a big surprise for him/her.

2 Likes / Preferences / Dislikes

A EXAMPLES (Read, Discuss and Practice)

Asking about Likes/Preferences/Dislikes

Do you like ice cream?
What do you like to do in your free time?
Do you like listening to classical music?
How do you like your new car?
Which do you like better, French or Italian bread?
How would you like to go for a walk along the waterfront?
Would you prefer tea of coffee?
Which would you prefer, going out or staying home?
Which would you rather eat, Chinese or Italian food?
Would you rather I read the report?
Don't you like American food?
What don't you like about Mrs. Johnson?
Do you dislike that painting?
What do you dislike about this book?
What do you hate about me?
What do you have against living in the country?

Expressing Likes/Preferences/Dislikes

I like you very much . . .
I love the sound of waves against the shore . . .
Don't you just love the way he speaks?
I have this thing for pistachio milk-shakes.
I'd prefer having margarine to butter.
I'd rather go shopping this afternoon.
I don't like the way he looked at my wife.
I dislike having to repeat everything I say.
I can't stand the sound of his voice.
I detest everything about the man.
He makes me sick.
I hate it when people insult me like that . . .

B MODELS (Read, Discuss and Perform the following model dialogues)

1 *A husband comes in and shows his wife his new haircut.*
   H: How do you like my new haircut?
   W: George! What happened to your hair? It's so short!
   H: Don't you like it?
   W: Well, it's different, to say the least . . .

CIE 1-H

2 *A salesman is talking with a middle-aged man and his wife.*
> **S:** I think you'll love this little car . . .
> **H:** Well, it's a nice-looking car. Do you like it, Milly?
> **W:** Yes . . . I do . . . but I'd prefer an automatic to a stick, to tell you the truth . . .
> **S:** Of course, you can have it with an automatic, if that's what you'd rather have . . . Would you like to test-drive it?
> **W:** I'd like to have my husband test-drive it first.
> **S:** Sure. Sir, would you like to test-drive it?
> **H:** Yes, I would. C'mon, Milly, let's go for a ride . . .

3 *Two factory workers are talking during break time.*
> **FW 1:** Jan, don't you like Mr. Edmonds? You're always fighting with him . . .
> **FW 2:** Quite honestly, I detest the man.
> **FW 1:** What do you have against him?
> **FW 2:** I really hate the way he gives orders. He makes you feel so small. I also dislike his bad temper . . .
> **FW 1:** I know what you mean. He isn't very sensitive, is he.

C SUGGESTED ACTIVITIES (Discuss and Perform)

If you were in the following situations, what would you do?

1 You're at a party talking with a sports-car enthusiast. You ask him/her about his/her likes and dislikes.
2 You're shopping for a shirt in a fashionable shop. The sales-person has taken out ten or fifteen. He wants to know which you prefer.
3 A couple are in a restaurant. The waiter brings the dessert cart and asks about preferences.

3 Interest / Enjoyment / Disinterest

A EXAMPLES (Read, Discuss and Practice)

Asking about Interest

How was your trip?
How did you find the movie?
What did you think of him?
Was the book interesting?
Did you find her interesting?
What's so interesting?
Are you interesting in skiing?
What kinds of interests do you have?

Asking about Enjoyment

Are you enjoying yourself?
Are you having fun?
Are you having a good time?
How's everything going?
Is everything O.K.?

Asking about Disinterest/Boredom

Are you bored?
You're not bored, are you?
Aren't you enjoying yourself?
Aren't you having fun?

Telling Somone to Be interested

Look interested.
Show an interest.
Don't act so bored.
Don't be such a bore.

Expressing Interest

Fascinating.
Very interesting.
I found it very interesting.
It was interesting to see it.
That sounds interesting.
I'm interested in music.
My interests include chess and photography.

Expressing Enjoyment

This is a great party.
I'm really enjoying myself.
I'm having a wonderful time.
I've never had this much fun before in my life.
It's been nice talking with you.
I enjoyed our conversation.

Expressing Boredom

I'm bored.
This party is boring.
What a drag this lecture is.
I'm bored out of my mind.
What a bore he is.

Telling Someone to Enjoy Themselves

Enjoy yourself.
Have fun.
Have a good time.
Have a blast.

B MODELS (Read, Discuss and Perform the following model dialogues)

1 *Two office workers are talking during break time.*
OW 1: You went to your first painting class last night, didn't you? How was it?
OW 2: Oh, it was really fantastic.
OW 1: What was so interesting about it?

OW 2: It was the first class, and we started by doing sketches of nude models . . . one man and one woman.
OW 1: That does sound interesting. Why did you begin with that?
OW 2: I guess the instructor was trying to get everyone interested in the class . . .

2 *A young man is having a job interview.*
   I: So, tell me, Victor. What interests do you have?
   YM: Well, I'm interested in a number of different things. For example, my interests include tennis, swimming, pottery, playing the saxophone, and other things . . .
   I: You're quite a well-rounded person, aren't you . . .

3 *A cocktail party host is talking with two guests.*
   H: So, Laura, are you enjoying yourself tonight?
   G1: I'm having a wonderful time, thank you.
   G2: So am I. This is a great party, Stan.
   H: I'm glad to hear that. Everyone does seem to be enjoying themselves, don't they…?
   G1: I'll say.
   H: Oh, Mark Temple just came in. Let me go welcome him. Enjoy yourselves.
   G2: Thanks. We will.

4 *Two managers are talking at an office Christmas party.*
   M1: How's it going, Vic?
   M2: Oh, O.K. This party's not much fun, is it?
   M1: I'm enjoying myself. Aren't you?
   M2: I don't know. I'm a little bored, I guess.
   M1: C'mon. You're just feeling a little down because it's Christmas and you're all by yourself. It happens to everyone.
   M2: Maybe that's it.
   M1: I'm sure it is. C'mon. Cheer up. Try and enjoy yourself.
   M2: Yeah. I will. Thanks.
   M1: That's O.K.

C SUGGESTED ACTIVITIES (Discuss and Perform)

What would you do in the following situations?

1 A couple are watching home movies at a neighbor's house. The husband is bored. The wife is being polite. The neighbors ask how they like them.
2 Two office workers are talking about a training session they attended that morning. It was a seminar on personal relations. Both had been to many similar ones before.
3 You're at a cocktail party. You're talking with another guest. You want to find out about how he/she likes the party and what kinds of things he/she is interested in.

4 Satisfaction / Dissatisfaction / Complaints

A EXAMPLES (Read, Discuss and Practice)

Asking about Satisfaction

How is your steak, Sir?
How do you like your room?
Is everything O.K.?
Is evertything satisfactory?
Are you satisfied with these photos?
Was everything to your satisfaction?
Did you find our service satisfactory?
Are you happy with your new suit?

Expressing Satisfaction

I really like my new haircut.
I'm completely satisfied with everything you've done for me.
It was satisfactory.
Everything is fine, thank you.
Everything was just perfect.
I'm happy enough with it.
It was O.K.
Not bad.
Good enough.

Asking about Dissatisfaction

Are you dissatisfied with something, Sir?
Was something not to your satisfaction?
What's the matter?
Do you have a complaint?
Do you want to complain about something?
What are you complaining about?

Expressing Dissatisfaction

I'm a little dissatisfied with the service here.
I'm a bit disappointed with the program.
The food was lousy.
I don't like the color.
I'm tired of working here.
I have a complaint.
I want to make a complaint.

Responding to Dissatisfaction/Complaints

I see.
I'm sorry to hear that.
I'll look into it.
I'll see what I can do about it.
I'll try and take care of it.
Be satisfied with what you have.
Like it or lump it.
Quit your bellyaching.
I'm tired of your complaints.
Stop your whining, will you?
What are you complaining about?

B MODELS (Read, Discuss and Perform the following model dialogues)

1 *A waitress asks a man and woman about their food.*
   Wa: Is everything O.K. here?
   M: Yes, thank you. Everything's fine.

Wa: Is your steak satisfactory?
M: Quite satisfactory.
Wa: How about your roast beef, Ma'am? Is it O.K. too?
W: It's just right. Just the way I like it.
Wa: Will there be anything else, then?
M: No. Not at the moment.

2   *A boy is complaining to his mother about his room.*
B: Hey, Mom. I don't like the new wallpaper in my room . . .
M: Well, that's just too bad. Be satisfied with it. I'm not going to change it now.
B: But it's dark for me to study in there now.
M: Now, Tommy, it was what you wanted. Like it or lump it. I'm not going to put up new wallpaper again for you.

3   *A woman is calling the Better Business Bureau.*
BBB: Good Morning, Better Business Bureau. Mrs. Sims speaking. Can I help you?
W: Yes. I'd like to make a complaint about a food processor I recently bought.
BBB: O.K. Just a minute please. Now, what is your complaint?
W: I bought a food processor last week and after I used it two or three times, it stopped working. When I took it back to the store, the manager told me that it broke because of my misuse, so they wouldn't take it back . . .
BBB: O.K., now, what exactly is wrong with the processor?

C SUGGESTED ACTIVITIES (Discuss and Perform)

How could the following situations be handled?

1   A man is being interviewed for a TV commercial. He went to a weight-loss clinic and lost 65 pounds.
2   Your room-mate always dirties the apartment and never cleans it.
3   You recently bought a new watch, but now it doesn't work. You're complaining to the store manager about it.

5 Wants / Hopes / Wishes

A EXAMPLES (Read, Discuss and Practice)

Asking about Wants/Hopes

What do you want?
Is there something you want?
Do you want to see Mr Paul?
Would you like to go too?
What would you like to do now?
What do you want me to do?
Whom do you wish to see?
Do you really hope to sail around the world in that?
Are you hoping to meet him after the show?

Expressing Wants/Hopes/Wishes

I want that green canary.
I want to kiss you.
What I want is peace and quite.
I would like to talk with you.
I'd like to ride the bus.
I want you to open this for me.
I wish to see Mrs Smyth.
I hope he comes on time.
I hope to sell it next week.
Here's hoping that you can do it.
Let's hope that he's there.
I wish that I could walk again.

B MODELS (Read, Discuss and Perform the following model dialogues)

1 *A young couple are talking during dinner.*
   H: Where do you want to go after dinner tonight?
   W: I'd like to take a walk along the waterfront.
   H: That's a good idea. Do you want me to bring the camera?
   W: O.K., but I don't want you to take any pictures of me. My hair looks terrible today.
   H: O.K. I promise I won't.

2 *A college student is talking with his uncle.*
   U: So, tell me, Emil. What do you hope to do after you graduate?
   CS: Well, I'm hoping to find a job in a small, progressive electronics company. But I also hope that it doesn't start until next September. I'd like to have the summer free, if I can.
   U: That sounds nice. I hope that everything works out O.K. for you.
   CS: Yeah. I hope so, too.

3 *Two neighbors are talking during a garage sale.*
   N1: How many people do you hope come to your sale today?
   N2: Well, I'm hoping that at least twenty-five or thirty people do. I wish that it didn't look like rain, though. If it begins to rain, people won't come.
   N1: Yeah. I wish it were nicer today, too. I'd go to the beach if it were sunny, but now I can't decide what to do . . .

C SUGGESTED ACTIVITIES (Discuss and Perform)

Think about what you would probably do in the following situations.

1 It is a rainy Sunday afternoon, and you are at a friend's place. You're both dissatisfied with your life, and you're talking about what you want to do instead.
2 You're a student, and you're talking with the job counselor at your school. The counselor asks you about what you want and hope to do in the future.
3 You're on a long camping trip and you're writing a letter to your boy/girlfriend at home.

6 Care / Concern / Unconcern

A EXAMPLES (Read, Discuss and Practice)

Expressing Care/Concern

What's the matter?
Are you all-right?
Is everything O.K.?
Is something the matter?
I'm worried about all of you.
I'm concerned about Dad.
I care about what you do.
I care that you're sick.
Take care of yourself
Take care, huh?

Asking for Care/Concern

Do you really care?
Does it really matter to you?
What do you care?
What does it matter to you?
Doesn't anyone care about me?
Nobody cares about me anymore.
Don't worry about little old me.
Do you care if I live or die?
Are you really concerned about my
well-being?

Telling Someone not to be Concerned

Don't worry about me.
I can take care of myself.
It's nothing.
Don't bother yourself about me.
This is none of your concern.
It's none of your business.
Stay out of my business.
Keep your nose to yourself.

Expressing Unconcern

Who cares?
I don't care.
What does it matter?
So what?
Who gives a damn?
What difference does it make?
The hell with it.
Screw it.

B MODELS (Read, Discuss and Perform the following model dialogues)

1 *Two friends are talking.*
   F1: Hey, Sally! How's it going?
   F2: Not so well.
   F1: Why? What's the matter?
   F2: I'm worried about my father. He's begun drinking again.
   F1: Oh, no. When did he start? Did something happen?
   F2: A few days ago. I don't know what happened . . .

2 *A father is talking to his son.*
   F: John, c'mon and sit down. I got a call from Coach Lane. He says you're getting into
      trouble at school lately.
   S: What do you care?
   F: What do you mean, "What do you care?" Of course I care.
   S: Do you really care? You're never home, you never show any interest in what I do . . .
   F: John, stop it. You know I'm busy. I have to earn money . . .

3 *Two people who share the same office begin talking.*
   P1: Is there something the matter, Chris? You look pretty down.
   P2: It's nothing.
   P1: C'mon. You can tell me.
   P2: Don't worry about it. It's none of your business.
   P1: Chris, I'm your office partner. I work with you . . .
   P2: I can take care of it myself.
   P1: O.K. If that's how you feel about it . . .

4 *T wo room-mates are talking.*
   RM 1: Mary, you got a call from Fritz before . . .
   RM 2: So what. Who cares.
   RM 1: He says he wants to apologize.
   RM 2: That's O.K. I don't care. It doesn't matter to me.
   RM 1: What happened? Did you have a fight or something?
   RM 2: No fight. He just insulted me in front of a lot of other people, that's all . . .

C SUGGESTED ACTIVITIES (Discuss and Perform)

What would you most likely do in the following situations?

1 You come home from work and find your daughter crying in the living-room.
2 A husband and wife are going out for the evening, and their teen-age son is baby-sitting with the younger children. The son tells them not to worry and to enjoy themselves.
3 A young woman receives a telephone call from an ex-boyfriend. He wants to get back together again after leaving her for another woman. She expresses her unconcern.

7 Sorrow / Regret

A EXAMPLES (Read, Discuss and Practice)

Asking about Sorrow/Regret

Are you sorry?
Do you feel sorry for Mr Johnson?
Are you sorry that you came?
Don't you feel any sorrow for the poor guy?
Don't you feel bad that you never spoke to him again?
Do you regret hitting her?
Don't you regret what you said to her?
Don't you have any regrets about what you did?
You have no regrets about having killed all those people?

Expressing Sorrow/Regret

I'm sorry.
I'm sorry about losing your radio.
I'm sorry that you couldn't get into the school you wanted to.
Let me say how sorry I am to hear that the operation failed.
I want to express my sorrow at failing you on this test.
I feel sorry for you.
I feel bad that I can't help you more.
I regret having to do this, but I must ask you to quit the club.
I regret to announce that tonight's show is cancelled.
I have my regrets about having quit school so young.

B MODELS (Read, Discuss and Perform the following model dialogues)

1 An office worker returns to work after his father's funeral.
OW 1: Welcome back, John. I'm sorry to hear about your father. It must be pretty rough on you.
OW 2: Yeah, it is. My Mom's taking it pretty hard, too.
OW 3: I can imagine. I'm sorry for you, too. You and your father were pretty close, huh?
OW 2: Yeah. We were . . .

2 A high-school teacher is talking with a student.
T: You know, you really hurt Linda's feelings before . . .
S: Yeah. I guess it was a pretty mean thing to say.
T: Are you sorry you said it?
S: Yeah. I sort of regret it. She really got me angry, but I shouldn't have said what I said.
T: Why don't you go and tell her you're sorry.
S: O.K. Maybe I will . . .

111

3 A TV interviewer is talking with a famous actress.
   I: So, tell us, Linda. Do you regret having left your family when you were so young?
   A: Yes, well, in some ways I regret having done so. On the other hand, I never would
      have been able to have a career in Schmaltztown.
   I: Have you ever been home?
   A: No, I haven't. That's something I do regret . . .

C SUGGESTED ACTIVITIES (Discuss and Perform)

If you were in the following situation, what would you do?

1 You meet a friend in a department store. He/she mentions that he/she was recently
   fired by his/her company.
2 A father comes home and finds his 5-year-old son crying in the living-room. He asks
   his wife, and she tells him the son was fighting with his little sister.
3 You recently sent an angry letter to a friend who disappointed you about something.
   You call your friend and express your regret.

8 Impatience / Annoyance

A EXAMPLES (Read, Discuss and Practice)

Expressing
Impatience/Annoyance

C'mon. Let's get started.
Let's go, huh?
Hurry up, will you.
I'm losing my patience with you, young lady.
I'm fed up with your demands.
You're driving me crazy.
*Stop pestering me.
You're bothering me.
You're annoying the hell out of me.
That man is impossible!
This is hopeless!
You're beyond belief!
*What a jerk he is.
What do you mean, "You can't come tonight?"
What are you trying to say?
*C'mon. Spit it out!

Telling not to be Impatient

Calm down.
Take it easy.
Don't be in such a hurry.
Don't get impatient.
Don't let it annoy you.
Don't be bothered by what he says.
Don't get your dander up.
Don't get so uptight.
Let's not get in an uproar.

B MODELS (Read, Discuss and Perform the following model dialogues)

1 *Two friends are getting ready to go out on a picnic.*
   F1: O.K. I'm almost ready. Just two more minutes . . .
   F2: C'mon. Let's get started. We were supposed to have met Alice twenty minutes ago.
   F1: I know. I know. Calm down.
   F2: What's taking you so long anyway?
   F1: I have to finish cleaning my camera . . .
   F2: Why didn't you do that before?
   F1: I forgot.
   F2: "I forgot." "I forgot." That's what you always say. You drive me crazy with your "I forgot"s.
   F1: O.K. O.K. Don't get uptight. I'm ready.

2 *A mother and daughter are shopping in a supermarket.*
   D: Mommy. Can I have a candy bar?
   M: No. I told you before. It's no good for you.
   D: But I'm hungry, Mommy.
   M: I don't care if you're starving. No. Stop pestering me.
   D: But Mommy . . .
   M: Lisa, I'm losing my patience with you . . .

3 *A woman and man are talking on the telephone.*
  W: . . . so, will you be ready by six?
  M: I'm sorry, Joan. I can't make it tonight.
  W: What do you mean, "I can't make it tonight"?
  M: Well, uh, uhmmm, . . .
  W: C'mon. What is it? Spit it out.
  M: I've, uhm, got another appointment tonight . . .

C SUGGESTED ACTIVITIES (Discuss and Perform)

How might you handle the following situations?

1 You just arrived in Los Angeles. You're at the airport trying to hail a taxi but none stop. A begger keeps coming up and asking you for money.
2 You are shopping in a large department store with a friend. You are waiting to be helped, but no one comes. Your friend is becoming more and more impatient.
3 You're looking for your watch. You thought you put it on the dresser in your bedroom. Your son comes in with a guilty look on his face. You ask him if he saw the watch, but he doesn't answer.

9 Indignation / Anger

A EXAMPLES (Read, Discuss and Practice)

Asking about Indignation/Anger

What's the matter?
What's happened?
What do you look so insulted about?
Why are you acting so insulted?
Did I insult you?
Are you angry about something?
Are you angry with me?
What are you so angry about?
You look pretty p-o'ed about something.

Expressing Indignation/Anger

Well, I've never . . .
I've never been so insulted in all my life.
Who are you to say such a thing to me?
Aren't you the pot calling the kettle black?
What do you mean I did a terrible job?
Are you trying to tell me I'm not good enough for you club?
Damnit!
Oh, hell!
You turkey!
You son of a . . .
You're getting me angry . . .
I'm starting to get angry . . .
1 . . . 2 . . . 3 . . . 4 . . .
Are you trying to make me angry?
*You piss me off.
You burn me up.

Telling not to be Angry

Calm down.
Take it easy.
Don't let it bother you.
Maybe you're a little too sensitive about
Don't be so touchy.
Don't be angry with me.
Temper, temper.
Let's try to hold our temper.
Don't get hot under the collar.
Getting angry won't help.

B MODELS (Read, Discuss and Perform the following model dialogues)

1 *Two office workers are talking in their office.*

OW 1: Hey, Marty, what's the matter? You look pretty angry about something. What is it?

OW 2: I tell you . . . I've never been so insulted in all my life.

OW 1: Why? What happened?

OW 2: I was just in to see the boss about my idea for making the office run a little more efficiently . . .

OW 1: Yeah . . .

OW 2: She said she wasn't interested, and didn't want to talk about it even.

OW 1: Well, don't let it bother you. It's not worth it.

OW 2: That's easy for you to say. You weren't insulted.

OW 1: Well, don't forget, she's having a pretty hard time now . . .

2 *A son comes in the house and talks with his father and mother.*
   S: Hey, Dad. I finished cleaning the yard. Can I go now?
   F: Wait a minute. Let me see. *(He goes to the window.)* Steve, that's a lousy job. Keep working on it.
   S: *(Angrily)* What do you mean it's a lousy job?
   F: *(More angrily)* It looks terrible. Look for yourself.
   S: I don't need to look. It's O.K. . . .
   F: Are you trying to tell me that that's the best you can do?
   M: *(Entering the room)* O.K. Temper, temper, you two. Calm down. What are you arguing about?

3 *A college student comes storming into the apartment.*
   CS 1: Oh, damnit!
   CS 2: What are you so angry about?
   CS 1: I'm late for my interview and my car won't start.
   CS 2: Well, getting angry isn't going to help. What's wrong with it?
   CS 1: I think the battery's dead . . .

C SUGGESTED ACTIVITIES (Discuss and Perform)

How might you handle the following situations?

1 You're waiting for a friend at a restaurant, and he/she is 40 minutes late, as usual. He/she finally comes in.
2 Two women are walking along the street and one bumps into a man coming from the opposite direction. He remarks that she's overweight and should watch where she's going.
3 You're going out on a date, you've just taken a shower, and you want to dry your hair. The hair drier doesn't work.

10 Disgust

A EXAMPLES (Read, Discuss and Practice)

Expressing Disgust

Euwh . . .
Yuck!
That's gross!
*You're disgusting.
That disgusts me.
I'm really disgusted by your bad jokes.
That's the most disgusting story I've ever heard.
What a disgusting thing to say to someone.
I'm disgusted with my job.

Asking about Disgust

Wasn't he gross?
Wasn't what he did disgusting?
Weren't you disgusted by everything that happened?
Isn't it disgusting how he follows her everywhere?
You must be pretty disgusted with yourself.
It must have been disgusting to see him like that.

B MODELS (Read, Discuss and Perform the following model dialogues)

1 *A little boy and a little girl are playing in the garden.*
B: Hey! Look what I found!
G: Euwh . . . Yuck. What is that?
B: It's a slug. Here, catch!
G: *(Screaming)* No. Get it away from me. It's disgusting.
B: C'mon. It's not so bad. Here, touch it.
G: *(Running away)* Stop it. Don't you dare throw that at me.

2 *Two people are talking on the way home from a party.*
P1: Well, how did you like Bill's little performance tonight?
P2: I thought he was really gross . . . drunk, telling dirty jokes and stories, and giving all the single women a hard time . . . Weren't you disgusted by him?
P1: Yeah, I was, too. That's certainly not the nicest way to behave in mixed company . .

3 *A man is finishing a joke with some friends.*
M: . . . and so he said. "You got it in there, now you get it out."
F1: Charlie, that's really gross.
F2: That's the most disgusting joke I've ever heard.
F3: Me, too. Where did you get that one from?
M: I heard it at the bar the other night . . .

C SUGGESTED ACTIVITIES (Discuss and Perform)

How could the following situations be handled?

1 You are walking in the park with a friend. You are not careful and step in some dog-doo.
2 Two elderly ladies are sitting in a bus station, and they see a young boy and girl kissing heavily in public on another bench.
3 You are listening to a story by a friend who was involved in a serious car accident.

Asking About / Stating I

CHAPTER 6

6

1 Belief / Trust / Disbelief / Mistrust

A EXAMPLES (Read, Discuss and Practice)

Asking about Belief/Trust
Do you think he's honest?
Do you believe she's guilty?
What do you believe are his reasons for coming here?
How can you believe that?
Are you convinced she's the most capable person?
Do you believe in yourself?
Don't you believe in freedom?
What do you believe in?

Asking for Belief/Trust
Believe me.
Believe me when I tell you I'll never leave you alone.
You'd better believe that he'd take advantage of you.
I swear to you that I'll love you to the end of the world.
You have my word on that.
Trust me.
Don't you trust me?
Have faith in me.

Stating Belief/Trust
I believe that he's innocent.
It's my belief that the killer was a woman.
I'm convinced that we arrested the right man.
I'm convinced of his ability.
I believe you.
I trust you.
I have complete faith in you.

Stating Disbelief/Mistrust
You're kidding.
That can't be.
That's unbelievable.
That's incredible.
*Nonsense!
I don't believe *you.*
Your story sounds fishy to me.
*Baloney!
*You're full of it.
I don't trust you.
I have no faith in you.

119

B MODELS (Read, Discuss and Perform the following model dialogues)

1 *A policeman is talking with a homicide detective.*
P: What do you think, Lieutenant? Do you believe his story?
D: I'm not sure whether to believe him or not. Part of it's believable. Part isn't. How about you? You believe him?
P: As for me, I'm convinced he's lying. How can a man not wake up when a gun goes off two feet from his ears?

2 *A man and woman are on their first date.*
M: Joyce . . . Please believe me when I say I love you. I do.
W: But, Will, how can I believe you. This is our first date . . .
M: I know. It's a little early in our relationship, but I'm convinced you're the woman for me.
W: Will, stop it now. What do you know about me?

3 *Two office workers are talking during their morning break.*
OW 1: So, what did he do after you said you didn't believe him?
OW 2: He tried to kiss me. There in the office.
OW 1: I don't believe it. What a jerk! What did you do?
OW 2: I slapped him. Then I said, "Mr. Benton, I don't believe in office hanky-panky, and please leave me alone from now on. I don't trust you, and if you try it again, I'll never come in alone after that."
OW 1: And what did he do then?

C SUGGESTED ACTIVITIES (Discuss and Perform)

What would you probably do in the following situations?

1 An acquaintance tells you he loaned a friend some money. You know the person in question and are suspicious of him/her.
2 You're a doctor, and you have to give an injection to a little boy who is extremely afraid. You try to reassure him.
3 A friend is telling you about a TV program where people do a lot of really strange things. He tells you a few of the things.

2 Certainty / Doubt / Reservations

A EXAMPLES (Read, Discuss and Practice)

Asking about Certainty/Doubt

Are you sure?
Are you certain?
Is that for sure?
Are you certain that we won't get into trouble?
Is it certain that they'll come on time?
How sure are you that it's a good idea?
Are you unsure about doing it?
Do you doubt my love for you?
Is there any doubt that he knows where it is?
You seem to have some doubts about my sincerity.
Do you have any reservations about signing this contract?
Do you have any qualms about doing business with him?

Stating Certainty/Doubt

Completely.
Absolutely.
I'm sure.
It's for certain.
I'm certain about it.
I'm certain that he didn't do it.
I have no doubt that he's O.K.
No doubt about it.
Rest assured, it's a good deal.
I'm a little uncertain.
I have some doubts about it.
I doubt he'll come.
I'm not so sure I trust him.
It's not certain that the train was in an accident.
I have some reservations about seeing him now.
There's something I have some qualms about . . .

B MODELS (Read, Discuss and Perform the following model dialogues)

1 *Two taxi-drivers are talking during lunch-time.*
   TD 1: Are you sure that this strike is a good idea?
   TD 2: I'm certain. Look, do you make enough money to live on?
   TD 1: No, I don't. That's for sure. But I doubt they're going to give us more money.
   TD 2: Why doubt it? If all of us strike, what can they do?
   TD 1: Is it certain that everyone will strike, though?
   TD 2: Some people are still undecided, sure. But they'll change their minds . . .

2 *Two students are talking about an upcoming test.*
   S1: Liz, do you think Professor Leyton is going to ask a question about the Industrial Revolution?
   S2: I'm sure of it. I doubt it'll be a difficult question, but there will be a question. Rest assured.

3 *Two business-people are talking at the hotel bar.*
   BP 1: Hey, there's something I want to ask you . . . You seemed to have some doubts about the Hedley contract. Why?

BP 2: Well, I've had quite a bit of contact with Herb Higgins, the VP there. I have some doubts about becoming very involved with or dependent upon him . . .

BP 1: Hmmm. I know what you mean. I'm not sure why, but I have some reservations about him, too. There's something I don't trust about him . . .

C SUGGESTED ACTIVITIES (Discuss and Perform)

How might the following situations be handled?

1 A friend tells you that he recently saw a former teacher who you thought was dead. He's certain but you have your doubts.
2 A husband and wife are leaving for their two-week vacation. The wife suddenly asks if they have turned everything off at home.
3 A salesman is trying to sell some unknown oil-company stock to a young man. The young man wants to be very careful.

3 Comments / Opinions

A EXAMPLES (Read, Discuss and Practice)

Asking for Comments/Opinions

How was the movie last night?
How do you like your economics class?
How does this report look to you?
Do you have any comments on this idea, Fred?
Is there anything you'd like to say about this issue?
Do you think that she was fair to him?
Do you feel that men always try to take advantage of women?
What do you think of this sales plan?
How do you feel about birth control?
What are your thoughts on this proposal?
What are your feelings on sex education in elementary school?
In your opinion, would Hal make a good branch manager?
What's your opinion on the way the President handled the crisis?
Could you give me your comments on the Mayor's decision?
I'd appreciate your comments on this paper I wrote.

Stating Comments/Opinions

It was a great lecture.
I really like your hair-do.
I think that what you did looks O.K.
I feel that there's a lot of injustice in America.
What I think is that we should look for a new sales plan.
In my opinion, capital punishment is needed in any society.
My opinion is that the movie was lousy.
As I see it, we're in for some hard times.
If you ask me, this test is a little too difficult.
If you're interested in my opinion, I think we should give up.
If I were you, I'd quit.
Let me say that your idea has some promise . . .

Reacting to Comments/Opinions

Thank you for your comments.
You're comments have been very helpful.
I really appreciate your comments.
I see.
I hadn't thought of that.
That's an interesting perspective.

Who asked you?
Who needs your comments?
Who asked you for your two cents?
Who are you to criticize me?
*Keep your opinions to yourself.
All you do is criticize me.
*Picky, picky.
Don't be a nit-picker.

B MODELS (Read, Discuss and Perform the following model dialogues)

1 Two people are talking during break time at the office.

P1: Tell me, Les. How do you feel about this new no smoking rule in the office?

P2: Quite frankly, I think it's a good idea. I smoke too much, and it might help me cut down.

P1: Hmmm. Well, as for me, I'm not sure I agree with it.

P2: Why is that?

P1: In my opinion, we all should have voted on it or something. I don't think management should have decided it.

2 A student asks another student to read something.

S1: Mary, I just finished this paper. Could you read it and give me your comments on it?

S2: Sure. I'll do it right now.

S1: *(Returning later)* Have you read it yet?

S2: Yeah.

S1: What do you think of it?

S2: The ideas are good. If I were you, though, I'd rewrite it in some places to make it clearer.

S1: Yeah. I thought so. Listen, thanks for your comments.

3 A wife and husband are talking in the kitchen.

H: You know, hon . . . That cake you made for the picnic today doesn't really look very good . . .

W: Who asked you for your opinion?

H: Well, I just thought . . .

W: Well, just keep your opinions to yourself . . .

C SUGGESTED ACTIVITIES (Discuss and Perform)

Think about what you might say and do in the following situations.

1 You have just gotten a haircut. You ask a friend for his/her opinion.

2 You are shopping downtown, and a TV newsperson wants to interview you about your ideas on population control.

3 An elderly couple are walking in the park. They see two young people kissing on a park bench.

4 Advice / Suggestions / Recommendations

A EXAMPLES (Read, Discuss and Practise)

Asking for Advice/Suggestions/Recommendations

Do you think I ought to call the police?
What do you think I should buy him for his birthday?
Do you have any ideas about how I can sell my car?
Should I try to talk with him about it again?
If you were me, what would you tell her?
If you were in my situation, would you forgive him?
What do you advise that I pack for the trip?
Do you have any advice for me?
Can you give me some advice about something?
How do you suggest that I fix this broken window?
Are you suggesting that I give up jogging?
What do you recommend I take for a bad headache?
Do you have any recommendations about a good hotel in Paris?
Can you recommend a suitable wine for dinner?

Offering Advice/Suggestions/Recommendations

I think you'd better start looking for a new job.
If I were you, I'd stop writing her.
It would probably be a good idea to send this by Express Mail.
Why don't you try calling her tonight?
How about taking the bus instead of driving?
Try ignoring her for a while.
I'd say that you'd better quit the team now.
I advise you to talk with your lawyer.
My advice is to be careful in doing business with them.
I suggest that we go out for a beer after the game.
Let me suggest that we buy a new copier.
I recommend that you cancel your appointment.
My recommendation is that we begin the sales program in May.

B MODELS (Read, Discuss and Perform the following model dialogues)

1 *A husband and wife are talking at breakfast.*
   W: Herm, this hair drier I bought yesterday isn't working. What do you think I should do about it?
   H: Why don't you try taking it back to the store?
   W: I was thinking of that, but I wanted to ask you first. Do you think you could look at it before I do?
   H: O.K., but not now. Maybe later.

2 *A student is talking with her advisor.*
   S: Mrs Wilson, what do you advise me to do about my chemistry class? Should I drop it or continue with it?
   A: I think it would be a good idea to talk with your instructor. Try talking with her about the problems, and see what she suggests.
   S: What if she says I should continue in the class?
   A: Then follow her advice. She doesn't want to fail you . . .

3 *Two neighbors are talking in their back yards.*
   N1: Hey, Jack. Got a minute? Can I ask you for some advice?
   N2: Sure. What's up?
   N1: I'm thinking about painting the house this summer. What kind of paint do you recommend?
   N2: I'd suggest a good water-base latex. It's easy to use and clean up. It's also relatively inexpensive.
   N1: That's what my father-in-law suggested. He recommended Duralux. Have you ever tried that?

C SUGGESTED ACTIVITIES (Discuss and Perform)

What would you do and say in the following situations?

1 You're going to make a cross-country trip but can't decide whether to go by bus, train or plane. You ask a friend.
2 Two college students want part-time jobs. They go to one of their teachers for suggestions.
3 A friend of yours is going out on an important date. He asks for recommendations about a good restaurant.

5 Purpose / Reasons / Plans

A EXAMPLES (Read, Discuss and Practice)

Asking about Purpose/Reasons/Plans

Why were you holding them hostage?
What were you trying to do when you called him a fool?
What did you hide the money for?
How come you cancelled your party?
What's your purpose in telling him that phoney story?
For what purpose did you try to interrupt me during the meeting?
What did you have in mind when you asked him for help?
Did you say that on purpose?
What do you intend to do to us?
Is it your intention to blackmail me?
For what reason are you selling your new car already?
What are you thinking of doing with those pictures?
Are you hoping to escape paying your taxes again this year?
Do you plan to go home during your summer vacation?
Do you have any plans for this week-end?
What are you planning to do tomorrow night?

Stating Purpose/Reasons/Plans

I helped her because she can help me sometime in the future.
I gave it to the police in order to keep it safe.
My purpose in inviting you here is to congratulate you.
Of course I did it on purpose.
I took the medicine so that I could get some relief.
I didn't mean to hit him so hard.
I intend to marry him, with or without your permission.
My intention was to destroy the papers before they were found.
I'm thinking of resigning from my job.
The reason why I called you is to ask you something important.
I hope to meet both of them in Las Vegas.
I'm planning to pay you next week.
What I plan to do is to get a divorce.
My plan is to invite him to dinner, get him drunk, and . . .

Hiding Purpose/Reasons/Plans

I've got no particular purpose in mind.
No reason in particular.
I'll never tell.
That's for me to know and you to find out.
You'll see.
It's a secret.

B MODELS (Read, Discuss and Perform the following model dialogues)

1 Two factory workers are talking during a break.
  FW 1: Hey, Stu. Mind if I ask you a question?
  FW 2: No. Go ahead. I don't promise to answer it.
  FW 1: How come you got into that fight with the boss the other day? What were you trying to do?
  FW 2: Oh, nothing in particular.
  FW 1: Aw, c'mon now. I know you better than that. You had something in mind. I could tell.
  FW 2: I did it in order to see how he would handle it.
  FW 1: Yeah? What for?
  FW 2: Just curiosity . . .

2 Two women are talking at a restaurant.
  W1: What do you intend to say to him when he gets home?
  W2: I intend to ask him how the lipstick got on his collar.
  W1: Do you think he'll tell the truth?
  W2: What are you going to do if he doesn't?
  W1: He'll tell me. Don't worry.

3 A student is talking with an uncle and aunt while visiting.
  U: Well. Mike. What are your plans for the future now that you've finished school?
  S: Actually, I don't have any particular plans. I'm not ready for college yet . . . I'm thinking of working a year or two to earn money . . . and get some experience . . .
  A: Those sound like pretty good plans to me, I must say . . .

C SUGGESTED ACTIVITIES (Discuss and Perform)

If you were in the following situations, what would you do?
  1 A friend is visiting your home and picks up something and breaks it on the floor. You are surprised.
  2 A young woman's father deserted the family when she was young. After years of searching, she found him and has his telephone number. She is calling him.
  3 It is Friday afternoon, and two secretaries are getting ready to leave the office. They ask each other about week-end plans.

6 Decisions / Choices

A EXAMPLES (Read, Discuss and Practice)

Asking about Decisions/Choices

Have you decided where you want to go for dinner?

Have you reached a decision?

Have you made up your mind about the stereo yet?

Have you figured out which one you want?

What have you decided to do?

What's your decision?

Have you chosen a partner?

Have you made a choice as to which one you want?

Which do you choose?

Have you changed your mind?

You're not going to change your mind are you?

Are you having second thoughts about this marriage?

Stating Decisions/Choices

I've decided that I'm going to quit my job.

I've decided to sell the car.

I've made up my mind.

My decision is to adopt Plan B.

I've made the decision to give up smoking.

What I've decided is that I'll postpone my decision.

I choose the small red box.

I want the blue one.

I've decided on beige.

I'll take the black-eyed one.

I've changed my mind.

On second thought, cancel my reservations.

Now that I think about it, I don't need this TV set.

B MODELS (Read, Discuss and Perform the following model dialogues)

1 *A husband and wife are talking during tea-time.*
   W: Tom, Darling. I've decided that I don't like the wallpaper in the living-room.
   H: Oh, that's nice, dear. What made you decide that?
   W: The living-room is always so dark. You can hardly see a thing in there in the evening.
   H: O.K. Then let's change the wallpaper. Go downtown and choose something tomorrow.
   W: I've already made my choice. What do you think of this?

2 *Two neighbors in an apartment building begin talking.*
   N1: I hear that Mr. Jacks has decided to raise the rent again.
   N2: So soon? When did he decide that?
   N1: Last week. I think it's unfair. I'm not going to pay it.
   N2: What choice do you have?
   N1: Well, we can fight it. If that doesn't work, we can always choose to move out.

3 *Two secretaries are talking during morning break.*
   S1: Well, today's the big day. You're actually going to go in and ask him for a raise.
   S2: Uhmmm . . . He doesn't seem to be in very good mood today, does he. Maybe I should wait . . .

129

S1: Are you changing your mind again? Yesterday you decided you'd do it today. Go ahead. Get it over with.

S2: On second thought, I don't need the money that badly.

C SUGGESTED ACTIVITIES (Discuss and Perform)

What would you probably do in the following situation?

1 You're considering buying a new car. A friend you told about your plans asks you about it.
2 Two neighbors are talking over their backyard fence. One is trying to decide whether to buy a swimming-pool.
3 You were going to go swimming with a friend today. However, you've changed your mind.

Asking About / Stating II

7

1 Ability

A EXAMPLES (Read, Discuss and Practice)

Asking about Ability

Can you open this bottle?
Are you able to read this?
Do you know how to fix a car?
Is it possible for a man to jump that high?
Do I have the ability to become a good painter?

Stating Ability

I can run faster than him.
I'm not able to swim.
I don't know how to make pottery.
It's possible to contact him, but it won't be easy.
You have the ability to do whatever you want.

B MODELS (Read, Discuss and Perform the following model dialogues)

1 *Two men are talking in front of a school door.*
   M1: John, I can't open this door. Can you?
   M2: Here, let me try . . . Wow! This door is really stuck, isn't it. Let's try pushing together . . .
   M1: O.K. One . . . two . . . three . . . Push!
   M2: Here it goes . . . slowly now . . .
   M1: Thanks a lot. I couldn't get it by myself . . .

2 *A young woman is taking an eye test at the eye doctor's.*
   ED: O.K. Miss Jones. Which is the smallest line you can read?
   W: Line five . . . It's E . . . P . . . B . . . H . . . I . . . N . . . W . . . .
   ED: That's very good. Are you able to read any of line six?
   W: I'll try . . . A . . . something . . . something . . . V . . . . I can't get the rest.
   ED: That's fine. Thank you.

3 *A young woman is talking with her art professor.*

W: Dr Rogers, do you think I have the ability to learn to paint? Or am I only wasting my time and money?

AP: What do you think, Mrs. Collins?

W: I don't know. I can't judge my own ability. Sometimes I feel good about it, other times I feel hopeless . . .

AP: That sounds like what any artist would say. How long have you been studying now?

W: Only four months. Maybe I'm expecting too much from myself.

AP: Perhaps . . . I think you have the ability to become a good artist . . . maybe not a world-famous one, but good.

C SUGGESTED ACTIVITIES (Discuss and Perform)

What would you do in the following situations?

1 You are a TV repairman. You are at a friend's house and the TV doesn't work.
2 You're walking along the ocean shore board-walk with a friend. You see a boat far out to sea.
3 A friend invites you to a swimming party, but you don't know how to swim.

2 Efforts / Attempts

A EXAMPLES (Read, Discuss and Practice)

Asking about Efforts/Attempts

Are you trying to upset me?

What are you trying to say?

Did you really try *to* get him to come to the meeting?

Have you attempted to sell your car in the wanted ads?

Did your attempts succeed or fail?

Are you really making an effort to get new members?

Were your efforts fruitful?

Stating Efforts/Attempts

I tried *to* call him, but . . .

I'm trying to find his number.

I'll try to buy that sweater for you today.

I'll see what I can do.

That was a nice try.

I attempted to calm her down, but I couldn't.

My attempts to see him failed.

I made an effort to fix it.

My efforts were indeed fruitful.

Urging to Try/Attempt

Try it.

Try drinking this.

Try and be on time next time.

Why don't you try buying a new car?

How about trying to look for a new job?

B MODELS (Read, Discuss and Perform the following model dialogues)

1 *Two businessmen are talking in the office.*

BM 1: What did you do when you saw you were going to be late?

BM 2: I tried calling Phil, but he had already left.

BM 1: Well, at least you made the effort to let people know . . .

BM 2: Yeah, but I'm afraid it wasn't enough . . .

2 *A college student sees a friend working on something.*

CS 1: What are you working on there?

CS 2: I'm attempting to fix this radio.

CS 1: Have you tried checking the battery contacts?

CS 2: No, I haven't. That's a good idea. Let me try that.

3 *A tennis player is talking with her coach.*

TP: Oh! I don't know what to do at this point. My serve just isn't going in . . .

C: Why don't you try sitting down and resting a while? Maybe you're trying too hard, and that's getting in your way.

TP: Do you think that will help?

C: Try it and see. You seem pretty upset right now . . .

C SUGGESTED ACTIVITIES (Discuss and Perform)

How might the following situations be handled?

1 A husband and wife are having an argument. Each claims the other never tries to understand him/her.
2 A friend is telling you that he/she is really interested in this other person, but that this other person never pays any attention to him/her.
3 You're talking with an acquaintance and mention you're catching a cold. Your friend suggests all kinds of remedies.

3 Possibility / Probability

A EXAMPLES (Read, Discuss and Practice)

Asking about Possibility/Probability

Is it possible to see Mount Fuji from here?
Is there any possibility of selling everything today?
What possibility is there that they're still alive?
What's the possibility of seeing Mr. Johnson today?
Can you come to my house tomorrow afternoon?
Will you be able to stop by the store on your way home?
Is there any chance we'll win the big game next week?
What are the chances of discovering the treasure?
How likely is an earthquake in the next five years?
What will probably happen to her?
What's the probability that it's going to rain tomorrow?
How probable is a war between the two countries?

Stating Possibility

Maybe.
Perhaps.
Could be.
It's possible.
He may visit here soon.
I might finish this today.
There's a good possibility that he'll get here on time.
There's a fifty-fifty chance that I'll go
Chances are they'll give up.
He'll most likely go home.
They will probably buy the car.
There's a 90 per cent probability of rain tomorrow morning.

Stating Impossibility

Impossible!
Not a chance!
No way!
That's totally out of the question.
It was impossible to see him.
It's not possible that he's still there, is it?
There's no chance of winning.
There is absolutely no possibility of staying here.
It's highly unlikely.

B MODELS (Read, Discuss and Perform the following model dialogues)

1 A man brings his camera to a repairer at a camera shop.
  R: Good morning, Sir. What can I do for you?
  M: Hi. I'd like to have this camera repaired. The shutter doesn't work.
  R: Here, let me see it . . . . I think it's possible to fix it.
  M: What are the chances of getting it back by the day after tomorrow?
  R: I'm afraid that's impossible. I'm closed both tomorrow and the day after tomorrow.

2 A young man is talking to a clerk at the stand-by counter of an airline.
  YM: Excuse me, Sir. I want to go to Boston. What's the possibility of getting a flight this afternoon?

135

C: Chances are you'll be able to. The 4 p.m. flight isn't full yet, so there'll probably be some empty seats.

3   *Two office workers are talking about the office picnic.*
OW 1: So tomorrow's the big office picnic, huh?
OW 2: Yeah. What's the probability it'll rain, do you think?
OW 1: I heard on the radio that there's only a 10 per cent probability of rain. It'll most likely be cloudy all day, though.

C SUGGESTED ACTIVITIES (Discuss and Perform)

Think about how you might handle the following situations.

1 You're out hiking with some people. You ask a friend if the path will continue to be as good as it is now.
2 A factory worker is planning to ask the boss for a raise. He's asking a fellow worker about the boss's reaction.
3 You're asking a neighbor what he/she will probably do during his/her next vacation.

4 Need / Necessity / Obligation

A EXAMPLES (Read, Discuss and Practice)

Asking about Need/Obligation

Is there anything you need?
Do you need something?
Are you in need of anything?
What need is there to say that?
Is there any need to quit?
Is it necessary to finish now?
What necessity is there to tell her about the decision?
Should I feed the baby now?
Ought I to find out her name?
Do I have to wash the dishes?
Am I Supposed to meet them?
Must we be nice to Mr Fontz?
Am I under any obligation to buy more magazines?
Are we obliged to help them?

Stating Need/Obligation

I need a screwdriver.
We need to talk about this.
There is a need for patience.
I can't do without you, baby.
It was necessary to scold him.
There is a necessity to lead the children by hand.
Calling ahead is a necessity.
I should tell you his name.
You ought to ask her soon.
You'd better do it today.
I'm supposed to guide you.
I have to clean the bathroom.
Dr Lee's got to help her.
Everyone must leave now.
I have an obligation to them.
You're obliged to tell him.

Denying Need/Necessity/Obligation

I don't need that wheelchair anymore.
There's no need to be insulting.
It's not necessary to give her everything she wants.
No need to worry about it.
Don't bother with it.
You needn't tell the whole truth.
We don't have to start this, this afternoon.
You shouldn't sleep with your mouth open.
You're not supposed to open that present now.
You ought not to use such bad language in school.
You're under no obligation to buy any more books.
There's no obligation to continue if you don't want to.

B MODELS (Read, Discuss and Perform the following model dialogues)

1 *A wife is going to go shopping.*
   W: Hey, hon. I'm going shopping. Is there anything you need?
   H: Yeah, just a minute. I'm working on the car, and I need a small can of spray paint. Can you get some for me?
   W: I think so. What color do you need?
   H: I'll write it down. I need a can of . . .

137

2 *A young man is filling out an application for a credit card. He addresses the bank clerk.*
YM: Excuse me . . . Is it necessary to fill out this part of the application form?
BC: No. There's no need to do that part. But you should fill in the bottom part and sign it . . .

3 *A wife and husband are talking while getting up.*
W: What do you want for breakfast?
H: Nothing. I don't have time. I've got to meet Fred and Jim at the golf course by 9 a.m. It's already 8.45.
W: Must you play golf today? Can't you just stay home?
H: Aw, hon . . . I've got no choice. We're supposed to talk about the new Bradley deal today . . .

4 *A boy is talking with a department store sales clark.*
C: . . . and here is your warranty card.
B: Do I have to fill it out right now?
C: No. No need to do it now. But, you ought to fill it out and mail it soon. That way, if your new computer game needs any repairs, the company will be under obligation to repair it or replace it for free . . .

C SUGGESTED ACTIVITIES (Discuss and Perform)

What would you do in the following situations?

1 You're at home making a pie. The recipe calls for four eggs, but you only have two. You call a neighbor.
2 A father is lecturing one of his children on the necessity for studying hard in school.
3 You invite a friend to a movie, but he/she declines because of a prior committment.

5 Logical Necessity

A EXAMPLES (Read, Discuss and Practice)

There must be a better way to do this.
I must have made a mistake.
This has to be the correct answer.
Those figures can't be complete.
Mr Frederick is sure to have received the letter by now.
We should be able to correct this problem easily.
This plan necessarily is rather complicated.

B MODELS (Read, Discuss and Perform the following model dialogues)

1 *A man receives a telephone call from a woman at his home.*
   M: Hello.
   W: Hello. Is this Mr. James Martin?
   M: Speaking.
   W: I'm calling from the Jones-Markham Insurance Agency. We have your life insurance ready for you now.
   M: There must be a mistake. I haven't ordered any life insurance.
   W: Aren't you Mr. James Martin of 1588 S. 18th Ave.
   M: No. You have the right name, but the wrong address.
   W: Oh I'm sorry. I must have looked up the wrong person.
   M: That's O.K.

2 *Two office workers are talking in the office.*
   OW 1: I can't understand it . . .
   OW 2: What's that?
   OW 1: I mailed a copy of the Kihens report to Martin Delmar at Fisk Inc., and he was supposed to have called as soon as he got it. It's sure to have reached there by now . . .
   OW 2: Why don't you try calling and find out?
   OW 1: Maybe I should . . .

3 *A woman is calling the electric company about her bill. She talks to a representative.*
   R: Good morning. Martinstown City Light.
   W: Hello. I just received my electric bill, and it can't be correct. It's for $130, and I wasn't home this month . . .
   R: O.K. I'll connect you with the Consumer Affairs Department. They should be able to help you. Could you please hold a moment?
   W: Yes. I'll hold.

C SUGGESTED ACTIVITIES (Discuss and Perform)

How would you handle the following situations?

1. You receive a bank statement which says that your checking account is overdrawn. You check your figures, but you can find no mistakes of yours.
2. You sent a package to a friend across the country, and 4 months later you get a call from him/her asking where it is.
3. A young bride is waiting in the church with her father and mother. The wedding was to begin at 2 p.m., and now it is almost 3.00 and the bridegroom hasn't come yet.

6 Prohibition

A EXAMPLES (Read, Discuss and Practice)

Prohibiting

I forbid you to open that letter.
You are forbidden to go out with that boy again.
I don't want you to ever come back here again.
You may not smoke in this office.
You must not talk loudly in the library.
It is forbidden to take antiques out of this country.
Smoking is prohibited in this part of the plane.

Asking about Prohibitions

May I sit in this section of the train?
Can we bring beer there?
Is it possible to put this notice up on the bulletin board?
Is camping permitted in this part of the park?
Am I forbidden to mention her name to him?
Is roller skating prohibited here?

B MODELS (Read, Discuss and Perform the following model dialogues)

1 A forest ranger finds some campers in a prohibited area.
    FR: Excuse me, folks. Camping is prohibited in this area.
    C1: Oh, we didn't know. We didn't see any signs.
    FR: There's a "camping prohibited" sign beside the road there . . .
    C2: O.K. We'll find another place. Can you recommend one?
    FR: There's a camping place about half a mile down the road.

2 A daughter is asking her mother for permission to go on a date.
    D: Mom, can I go out with Stanley tomorrow night?
    M: Tomorrow is Wednesday, isn't it? No. It's a weeknight.
    D: Oh, Mom. It's O.K. I'll finish my homework early.
    M: No. I forbid you to go out.
    D: Mom, why?
    M: You know the rules in this house. You may not go out on a weeknight. That's final.
    D: Oh, Mom. You never try to understand, do you . . .

3 A man, who is waiting in a doctor's office, talks with the nurse.
    M: Excuse me, Miss. Is smoking permitted here?
    N: I'm sorry, Sir. It isn't. You can smoke outside if you want.
    M: O.K. Thanks.

CIE 1-K

C SUGGESTED ACTIVITIES (Discuss and Perform)

How might the following situations be handled?

1 You are sitting in the non-smoking section of a plane. The person next to you takes out a cigarette and lights it.
2 You are driving in a national park, and you see an interesting back road. You begin to drive up it, and a forest ranger steps into the road and signals you to stop.
3 You were on vacation in a foreign country, and you bought some valuable artifacts. You are at the country's customs inspection. The customs officer won't let you leave with them.

7 Hypothetical Situations

A EXAMPLES (Read, Discuss and Practice)

Future Hypothetical Situations

If you like the car, will you buy it?
I'll kill him if he doesn't bring the money.
If you go, I go too?
If he has forgotten your name, will you try to talk with him?
Suppose I can't go. Will you go instead of me?
Let's suppose he's not sick. Are you going to fire him?
I'm going to go even if I don't get time off from work.
What will you do in the event that you find him?
Given that you can't find the papers, what will you do?

Present Hypothetical Situations

If you loved me, you would buy this for me.
Would you be here now if I hadn't called you?
What would you be doing now if you were living in San Francisco?
If I were to answer that question, would I get into trouble?
If I were you, I'd forget that I ever saw him.
Were you to give me the money, I'd free her.
Would you still love me even if I didn't have any money?
Suppose you weren't poor. Would you still be in love with her?

Past Hypothetical Situations

I would have talked with him if I had had the time.
If you hadn't been talking so much, you would have seen the fire.
If you had been me, what would you have done?
Had the police arrived in time, they would have caught the thief.
Would you have begun talking with me even if I was ugly?
Suppose you had seen him, would you have become so angry?
What would you have done in the event that everyone had been sick?

B MODELS (Read, Discuss and Perform the following model dialogues)

1 *A husband and wife are talking at dinner.*
   H: Jan, did you hear the weather report for tomorrow?
   W: Yeah. The report said that it's going to snow tonight, perhaps 5 – 10 inches. How will you get to work tomorrow if it snows?
   H: If it's snowing, maybe I'll have to take the bus.
   W: What if the buses aren't running?
   H: If the buses are shut down, they'll probably close the factory.

2 *A young man is asking a friend for some advice.*
   YM: . . . I don't know what to do about this contract, Doug. What would you do if you were me?
   F: Well . . . What would happen if you didn't sign it? Would they fire you?
   YM: I don't know what they would do . . .

3 *Two housewives are talking about their women's club.*
   H1: Are you going to run for club president this time?
   H2: I'm not sure. Suppose I were to run. Do you think I could win?
   H1: I think you'd have an excellent chance of winning.
   H2: Do you think I could even if Marge decided to run again?
   H1: I'm sure of it. People are pretty dissatisfied with Marge. Were you to announce your intention to run soon, you'd definitely win . . .

4 *Two friends are talking at a local bar.*
   F1: . . . I just can't believe I missed such a great opportunity. If I hadn't been so drunk, I could have brought those diamonds at a real steal . . .
   F2: Yeah, well, look at it this way: suppose you hadn't been so drunk. Would you have begun to talk with him?
   F1: No. I suppose not. You have a point there.

5 *Two persons are talking in a restaurant.*
   P1: C'mon, Jean. Stop blaming yourself for the accident. It wasn't your fault.
   P2: But if I had only been more careful, maybe it wouldn't have happened . . .
   P1: Accidents happen. You can't blame yourself for everything that goes wrong in the world.
   P2: But if I had just told Billy to put on his seat-belt, he might have lived . . .

C SUGGESTED ACTIVITIES (Discuss and Perform)

If you were in the following situations, what would you do?

1 Two sales-people are considering different ways to sell encyclopedias.
2 You and a friend are talking about what you would be doing now if you hadn't made certain decisions in the past.
3 An elderly couple are looking back on their lives and talking about what would have happened if . . .

8 Conditions

A EXAMPLES (Read, Discuss and Practice)

I'll go if you go.
I'll try to meet him tomorrow, if possible.
I'll only do it if you help me.
He will not write the report unless you order him to.
The professor will co-operate on the condition that we pay him overtime.
I'll talk with him provided that he doesn't insult me again.
You can sell this if and only if you promise to split the profit with me.

B MODELS (Read, Discuss and Perform the following model dialogues)

1 Two college students are talking in their dormitory room.
S1: Les, are you going to go to the dance at the student center tonight?
S2: I don't know. I'll go if you go, but I don't want to go by myself. Are you going to go?
S1: I'm hoping to. But I can only go if Mr. Johns lets me out of work early tonight.
S2: What are the chances that he will?
S1: In the event of business being really slow the chances are he will. If we're busy, he won't. The problem is that I can't be sure until the last minute.
S2: That's O.K. As I said, I'm not going unless you do. I hate those parties if I'm by myself . . .

2 A man is talking with a used-car salesman.
S: Well, Mr. Johnson. Here's the bill of sale.
M: O.K. Let me read it first, though . . .
S: It's a standard bill of sale. There's nothing to worry about at Honest Abe's . . .
M: Well, I never sign anything until I've read it first.
S: Suit yourself . . .

3 A young man and woman are talking in a small restaurant.
YM: Marge, are you sure you won't come home with me this week-end?
W: Well . . . I'll go on the condition that we only stay for a few hours. Your mother and I begin to get on each other's nerves when we're together too long.
YM: O.K. That sounds fair.
W: And one more thing. I'll go if and only if you promise not to take automatically your mother's side if there's an argument.
YM: O.K. O.K. I promise . . .

C SUGGESTED ACTIVITIES (Discuss and Perform)

What would you do if you were in the following situations?

1 You and a friend are at the community swimming-pool. You are both on the high dive, and he/she suggests jumping off. You don't want to be the first.

2 A husband and wife have had a fight. She is with her family. They are talking on the phone, and he wants her to come home. She is stating her conditions.
3 A boy is asking his father for permission to use the family car. The father is making the son agree to certain conditions.

Appendix 1

Preliminary Activities

1 Circle-Square-Triangle/Line-Ups
2 Mirror Reflection
3 Scene or Story-building
4 Visualizations
5 Sensations and Feelings

During the first few class-meetings and at the beginning of each class, you can prepare students for the types of activities they will be involved with in class. The following exercises will help to do so in two ways: instruction-following and imagination-using. Some of them have the students following and giving the kinds of instructions they will need to understand and use while practicing and performing. Other exercises have the students use their imaginations to think of various ways to see and do things, to recall sensations, feelings and actions, and to create scenes, situations and characters in their imagination.

1 Circle-Square-Triangle/Line-Ups

This is a well-known exercise which begins with the teacher asking the students to stand in a group in the center of the room. The teacher then requests them to stand in a circle, without speaking. Using a variety of non-verbal means, students have to communicate which one another in order to form themselves into the requested shape. Some people will probably want to talk, and they should be reminded not to. Next, the teacher can ask everyone to change the circle into a square, again without saying anything. After forming the square, the teacher might request a triangle, then a circle or square again. If there are a lot of people, the teacher might ask them to spell out a word — like CAT or BUS.

Another version of this exercise involves the teacher asking students to stand in a line according to height, again without speaking. They are then requested to line-up according to month and date of birth: with January 1 at one end and December 31 at the other end of the line. Again, students must do this without speaking. If you want to, you can ask them to line up by first letter of last name, number of years of English study, or other ordered bases.

These exercises require a non-verbal communication system, co-operation and some people taking leadership responsibilities in order to successfully accomplish them.

2 Mirror Reflection

In this fairly well-known exercise, the teacher asks one student to join him or her and to act like a mirror. This means that the student must reflect like a mirror any actions that the teacher performs. For example, the teacher may do some simple things like bending over and touching toes, squatting, grimacing, slowly rising, stretching, yawning and so on. The student must do the same things at the same time, in mirror fashion. The two roles can be switched, with the student performing the actions and the teacher reflecting them. Two students can then be asked to do this together, or the class can be divided into pairs, with one person performing a sequence of actions and the other reflecting it.

These exercises involve physical activity, co-ordinated movement and people having fun.

3 Scene or Story-building

In this exercise, the teacher instructs students to act out certain everyday-life activities. You may give instructions, or you or the students may be telling a story while one or more people act out the activity. Scene or story-building can involve such activities as: making breakfast, writing and mailing a letter, going to the dentist, helping in an accident or something similar.

The actors follow the instructions or the story-line, imagining whatever props or other people are necessary. An example of directions you might give for a simple situation are:

1 Go to the kitchen.
2 Open the refrigerator.
3 Take out a carton of milk.
4 Go to the cupboard and take out a glass.
5 Open the milk carton and pour some milk in the glass.
6 Close the milk carton and put it away.
7 Take a sip of milk.
8 Drink down the whole glass at one time.
9 Burp loudly and smile.
10 Go to the sink and wash out the glass.
11 Put the glass in the dish-drainer.
12 Leave the kitchen.

This exercise requires students to follow instructions or a story-line and to use their imagination. It is easy for the people acting because they don't really have to say anything, unless they are given something to say by the people giving instructions or telling the story.

4 Visualizations

In this exercise, you create multi-sensory pictures in the mind: combining sights, sounds, tastes, smells, touch. Visualizations vary in complexity and action. An example might be:

O.K., everyone. Please close your eyes. Relax and close your eyes. Close them gentle and relax. Now I want you to see a picture of a box. You see a small box. The box is wrapped in blue paper. There is a ribbon around the box. It is a red ribbon. There is a yellow bow on top. You see a small box wrapped in blue paper. It has a red ribbon with a yellow bow on top. The box is on a table. The table is in your home. You are sitting at the table. You are looking at the box. You want to open the box. You are at home, sitting at the table, looking at the box. You want to open it. You take off the bow. You take off the ribbon. Now you slowly unwrap the paper. You can hear the paper. The paper is making a crinkling sound. Now the paper is off the box. You begin to open the box. You look inside it. You see a child's toy inside. It has a pleasant smell. You take out the toy and begin to play with it. You are playing with it.

Now, I want you to come back to the class-room. You hear my voice. You hear other sounds in the room. You are in the room. Now, open your eyes . . .

You can talk about a number of things after the visualization: the size of the box, the room where you were, the toy that was in the box, and so on.

In preparing visualizations, it is important to create scenes or story-lines that are specific enough to focus on, but general enough to fit within everyone's imagination. The key is to find common cultural or human experiences, and to build around those. It is also a good idea to prepare students for any new or unusual vocabulary ahead of time, because it's very hard to do that within the visualization.

This exercise helps build the ability to imagine the people, situations and settings that will be necessary in later activities when the students perform the Examples, Models or Suggested Activities for each lesson.

5 Sensations and Feelings

In this exercise, learners are asked to remember situations where they experienced certain physical sensations or emotions. These can be such things as: feeling cold, feeling hot and sweaty, feeling tired, having a stomach-ache, feeling angry or lonely or happy or afraid and so on. They are asked to recall the situation and, in particular, how the sensation or feeling showed itself in their behavior. People can be helped to recall the sensations or emotions through a series of questions, such as:

Can you remember a time when you felt really ....?
When was it?
Where were you?
Were you alone or with other people?
What were you doing? What were other people doing?
What happened to make you feel that way?
How did you show that you were ....?

The first time through, it's best to work with physical sensations and pleasant emotions. Once the students become familiar with the exercise, they will generally select experiences that reveal as much, or as little about themselves, as they want to when they talk about them afterwards. Working with emotions such as anger, disappointment, depression, jealousy, etc., can be a little problematic. However, they can also contribute to a very special group feeling if everyone involved has a sensitivity towards and a sincere interest in working with and helping one another.

This exercise works on the more effective elements in practicing and performing the "Examples, Models and Suggested Activities." The activities in Appendix 2 can also be used for practicing and performing the "Examples, Models and Suggested Activities." An important point is that people should not be asked to act out physical sensations and emotions. Rather, they should be asked to remember how they felt when they experienced a particular sensation or emotion, and they should try to put that feeling into what the're saying and doing. In so doing, the practising and performing will be more "genuine", and the genuineness will help people learn what it is important to learn in the "Practice and Perform" parts.

Appendix 2

Suggested Techniques

1 Interpretative Reading
2 Talk and Listen
3 Skits/Improvised Role-Playing
4 Puppet Shows
5 Tape-recording and VTR
6 Plays

The six techniques explained in Appendix 2 can be used in the "Practice and Perform" stages of the "Examples, Models, and Suggested Activities". You can use them to help students actively learn the things they've read, thought about and discussed in previous stages. Since all of these techniques involve students actively working with other students, it is a good idea to prepare students for these techniques by using the preliminary activities explained in Appendix 1.

1 Interpretative reading

Simply stated, interpretative reading is reading a line, script or story in the way that a particular person in a particular situation would say it. You read it with the same intonation, stress, emotional quality and speed as that person would use. There is no physical movement with interpretative reading. The reader sits or stands in one place. Everything is conveyed through the reader's voice and the intonation, stress, emotional quality and speed that the reader uses.

Interpretative reading can be used to practice or perform the "Examples, Models, or Suggested Activities". In the "Examples" section, after students understand the meaning and context of the examples, you can ask them to interpretatively read the examples. Similarly, after the models have been read and discussed, you can ask one or more students to interpretatively read the models. Lastly, if you have asked students to write skits in the "Suggested Activities" section, you can ask them to read these interpretatively before they actually perform them.

Success in using this technique depends on students understanding the meaning and context of things said in the "Examples and Models". If they don't understand the meaning of certain words or expression, or if they don't understand the time, place, people, people's intentions and feelings, it will be very difficult to do interpretative reading. If these things have become clear in the "Read and Discuss" stages, students will have much less difficulty. In addition, the more they use and get used to the technique, the better they become at it.

2 Talk and listen

Richard Via, in his book *English in Three Acts**, discusses "Talk and Listen" as a technique actors sometimes use to learn parts in a play. The procedure involves the following things:
- (a) dividing a dialogue or script into parts and writing the different parts on separate cards or pieces of paper,
- (b) performers looking at and listening to the other person while the other person is speaking,
- (c) the performer's establishing eye-contact with the other person when the performer is speaking to the other person.

Of course, it is important that the performers understand the time, place, people, peoples intentions and feelings, of the situation. These things should become clear during the "Read and Discuss" stages of working with the lessons.

"Talk and Listen" cards might look as follows:

Dialogue (from Chapter 1, Lesson 2)

A branch manager is meeting a vice-president at the airport.
BM: Good afternoon, Mr. Browning. Welcome to Martinstown.
VP: Thank you, Les.
BM: How was your flight?
VP: Oh, not bad. It was a little rough in places, but . . .

Talk and Listen Card 1

A branch manager is meeting a vice-president at the airport.
BM: Good afternoon, Mr. Browning. Welcome to Martinstown!
VP:
BM: How was your flight?
VP:

Talk and Listen Card 2

A branch manager is meeting a vice-president at the airport.
BM:
VP: Thank you, Les.
BM:
VP: Oh, not bad. It was a little rough in places, but . . .

*Via, Richard A. *English in Three Acts* The University of Hawaii Press, 1976.

The reason for putting the two parts on two separate cards is to provide students with some help but, at the same time, to prevent them from just reading the lines without listening to the other person. When students are performing, they should not be reading the cards: they should be looking at and listening to each other. The cards serve as memory jogs, so that memorizing the dialogues is not necessary. The substitution of alternative ways to say the same thing are fine, as long as they are appropriate to the situation. Students can also be encouraged to continue the situation beyond what is on the card.

Via points out that if people are not listening to each other, you can get them to listen closely by changing a part to make it incongruous. For example, if the person playing the businessman's part above is not listening, you can change the vice-president's part like this:

Talk and Listen Card   2

A branch manager is meeting a vice-president at the airport.
BM:
VP: My name isn't Browning. And who are you?
BM:
VP: I told you my name isn't Browning. You're making a mistake.

3 Skits/Improved Role-Playing

Skits and improvised role-playing can be used with the "Suggested Activites" section of each lesson. In doing skits, students discuss and write out scripts for the situation. They then use the scripts in performing. In doing improvised role-playing, students discuss the situation and then perform it without writing scripts. Skits can be useful first steps to improvised role-playing, or can be used if the situation is rather long and complicated. Improvised role-playing more closely approximates the ability to use what they're learning in everyday life outside of class and, thus, are a more valuable type of exercise.

As with interpretative reading and Talk and Listen, students need a good understanding of the context of the situation: the time, place, and people's intentions and feelings. If students have a clear image of the situation and people and people's behavior, they'll be able to perform more naturally and creatively. For this reason, working on the preliminary activities given in Appendix 1 will be a great help to students when they reach the "Practise and Performing" stages in the "Examples, Models, and Suggested Activities".

4 Puppet Shows

Sometimes students find it easier or an interesting change of pace to perform the "Models of Suggested Activities" using puppets as the performers. This is especially true if there are many people who feel uncomfortable about performing for any of a number of reasons we sometimes can do nothing about. With puppets, they can use the language without actually being "on stage". They are, instead, the hidden animators and voices.

Puppets can be used as simple or elaborate as time, resources and funds allow. Puppets can be made from old socks, cut out from paper or paper plates, or they can be bought commercially. Stages can be constructed from cardboard boxes or drawn upon a blackboard. The puppeteers can be hidden or visible. Left to their own ingenuity, students usually come up with a lot of imaginative things without a lot of help from the teacher.

5 Tape-recording and VTR

After students have begun to feel comfortable with the performing stage, you can begin using tape-recording or VTR, if available. It is often a little threatening to try to use these from the beginning, unless students have some prior experience working with them. However, as time goes on, taping or video taping can provide an interesting change of pace as well as a feeling of excitement and accomplishment. Hearing and seeing themselves on tape will provide students with interesting things to talk about, questions to ask, and sheepish grins and nervous laughs. One of the other added benefits is that the tapes can be saved, with good performances by one class being used as materials for subsequent classes.

6 Plays and productions

One other technique to consider if time and circumstances permit is putting on a play or production. Most of the functional elements covered in this volume can be found in most plays. In this way, students will not only learn how these things are used in somewhat isolated situations, but also how they fit into the overall flow of events in a story or life.

If both teacher and students find the thought of a play or production an interesting one, more information about this subject can be found in Richard Via's *English in Three Acts,* * mentioned earlier. Via goes into depth about the things you'll need to take into account if this is a direction you want to go. It is also an excellent resource on the application of drama approach and techniques to language training.

---

*See also: Via Richard and Larry E. Smith, *Talk and Listen,* Pergamon Press, 1983.
Romijn, Elisabeth and Convee Seely, *Live Action English,* Pergamon, 1981

Index of Functions

Printed in Great Britain by A. Wheaton & Co. Ltd, Exeter